Liste[n &]
French

BY LEON J. COHEN

Goshen Central School

Goshen, New York

and

The Editorial Staff of

DOVER PUBLICATIONS, INC.

DOVER PUBLICATIONS, INC.
NEW YORK

Copyright © 1956 by Dover Publications, Inc.

Published in Canada by General Publishing Company, Ltd., 30 Lesmill Road, Don Mills, Toronto, Ontario.

Published in the United Kingdom by Constable and Company, Ltd., 10 Orange Street, London, WC 2.

Standard Book Number: 486-20875-3

Library of Congress Catalog Card Number: R60-113

Manufactured in the United States of America
Dover Publications, Inc.
180 Varick Street
New York, N. Y. 10014

CONTENTS

4   **CONTENTS**

INTRODUCTION

The Plan and Presentation of "Listen and Learn"

Listen and Learn French is an introductory course designed to give you in spoken and written form the basic sentences, phrases, and vocabulary that you will need in almost every travel situation. The course does not pretend to teach the grammatical structure of French through a series of progressive and graded lessons. You will, however, absorb much of the structure of the language in the natural way you first learned to speak English as a child. You need not start at the beginning; listen and learn whatever sections interest you. Although a systematic study is probably most desirable, don't feel obliged to master any series of phrases before going on to the next. This course differs from most others because whatever you learn will be useful, regardless of your previous study, your rate of forgetting, your length of study.

You will observe that *Listen and Learn French* is a straightforward course designed to help you solve real travel problems. Its value rests as much on what is omitted as on what is included. You will find "Give me small change" (an urgent need in foreign travel), but do not look for "This is the pen of my aunt."

Listen and Learn French teaches you what *you* will say, not what you will hear. This plan is a deliberate editorial policy, based on travel experience which proves that no editor can possibly anticipate the exact form in which your question will be answered. A waiter can be anything from taciturn to over-talkative. He may answer your question by a silent nod or by voluble news of his cousin in Toledo. The editors have, therefore, framed most questions and statements

5

to elicit a simple response that will probably contain the very words in your question.

The section on making yourself understood (entries 40–52) will come to your aid in achieving comprehension. Phrases such as "Please speak slowly," "I speak only a little French" are essential because the reasonably good pronunciation that you will achieve through imitation will often suggest a greater comprehension of the language than you may actually have.

Method for Study—The Records

In the recordings, each phrase is spoken in English and in French followed by a pause sufficient to allow for repetition. After some practice you may wish to use this pause to anticipate the next phrase and check your pronunciation against that of the speaker. If you first listen to the record while following the text, you will find the separate study of record and text more meaningful. Play the record whenever you have an opportunity, while working, engaging in a hobby—whenever you are within listening range of a record player. Although active participation is best, even passive but repeated listening will familiarize you with useful French.

Method for Study—The Manual

The *Listen and Learn French* manual is complete in itself and is designed so that you can carry it in your pocket for unobtrusive reference and study. Read it at odd moments—while commuting, eating, waiting— and try to learn 10 to 15 words and phrases a day. Test your pronunciation against the records. In 30 to 60 days you will know the language essential for travel.

Of course, you will take the manual with you when you go abroad. All that you have learned will be available to you for reference and refresher study. You will find the extensive index on pages 149–158 especially helpful. Notice that each entry in the book is numbered and that the index refers to these numbers. The indexing method enables you to locate information quickly and without searching the whole page.

Use the index to test yourself. It contains every important word and phrase that you have learned in the *Listen and Learn French* course. Test your vocabulary and your ability to form phrases and questions from the words in the index.

Speak French When You Travel

When you travel abroad, do not be timid about using what you have learned. The native listener is always pleased and flattered when you attempt to speak his language. Whether this is your first trip or your twenty-first, your native listener will know that you are an American (years of intensive study will never disguise this fact) and he is ready to accept pronunciation and grammar that is less than perfect. So do not be self-conscious if your speech is halting and awkward. Speak up, politely, and clearly. Timid mumbling may be a greater barrier to comprehension than faulty nasalization. Remember that your purpose is to communicate, not to pass as a Frenchman.

The *Listen and Learn French* course will enable you to communicate on a simple but very practical level. You will make yourself understood on practical everyday matters. With time and further study, improvement will come and the range of your conversation will expand. Do not, however, let your present inability to discuss French drama or the current political scene inhibit you from asking questions in French. You know your own language limitations and you must speak French in spite of them and within them.

Bear in mind that your French listener is not judging or grading you. He is kindly disposed toward you and is equally interested in trying to communicate. When you make yourself understood in French you have achieved your purpose. If you are interested in a grade, score yourself 100%.

Speak the French you have learned in *Listen and Learn French*. The effort will not only make your travel more exciting and rewarding but will also contribute to better foreign relations. Too many Americans go abroad demanding that all peoples of the world speak English—an attitude that non-Americans find narrow and condescending. If you are willing to meet and speak to people in their own language and on their own level, you may not impress the Frenchman with your command of the French subjunctive, but you will create an impression more representative of the warmth, open-mindedness, and democratic feeling of America. This impression may be more valuable than thousands of words of propaganda.

FURTHER STUDY

After you have mastered the material of *Listen and Learn French* you may wish to continue with more formal study in order to become more fluent in speaking, reading, and writing. It is entirely possible to carry on study by yourself with a few well-selected books and with such audio-visual aids as French movies and French radio broadcasts.

The following books are not expensive and can be purchased through your local dealer for the publisher's current (1967) list price.

Dictionaries

Larousse's French-English, English-French Dictionary. Pocket Books, 630 Fifth Ave., New York, N.Y. 10020. 25,000 entries. 526pp. $0.75. Pocket size. Will answer most needs. You will do well to purchase this book or the title below immediately.

Collins French-English, English-French Gem Dictionary edited by Gustave Rudler and Norman C. Anderson. William Collins Sons and Co., Ltd., 215 Park Ave. S., New York, N.Y. 10016. 32,625 entries. 760pp. $1.25. Sturdier and somewhat more convenient than *Larousse.*

Cassell's French-English, English-French Dictionary. Funk & Wagnalls Co., 360 Lexington Ave., New York, N.Y. 10017. 128,200 entries. 1312pp. $7.50. Standard desk-size dictionary. It is too large for travel but valuable for study and reference.

Introductory grammars

New Fundamental French by Wilson Micks and Olga Longi. Oxford University Press, 417 Fifth Ave., New York, N.Y. 10016. 320pp. $4.25.

If you studied French in high school or college, or if you have some grasp of the general principles of grammar, you will find the following review-type books helpful.

Unified French by Louis Sorieri. Oxford Book Co., 71 Fifth Ave., New York, N.Y. 10003. *Two Years*, $1.20; *Three Years*, $1.45 paperbound.

French Grammar by Francis M. du Mont. Barnes and Noble, Inc., 105 Fifth Ave., New York, N.Y. 10003. 277pp. $1.50 paperbound.

Readers

Graded Readers by Bond and others. D. C. Heath & Co., 2700 N. Richardt Ave., Indianapolis, Ind. 46219. Twenty elementary ($1.00) to intermediate ($1.08) readers are available paperbound.

Novels and general literature

Your local book dealer or college store probably has a good selection of foreign language books and a visit to him will be rewarding. You will find many items that are inexpensive. The following list of specialist dealers have a more extensive stock ranging from elementary to very advanced. They will send you catalogs and announcements if you drop them a card.

New York, N.Y.
Adler's Foreign Books, 110 W. 47th St., 10036.
Barnes and Noble, Inc., 105 Fifth Ave., 10003.
French Book Center, 31 W. 46th St., 10036.
French Book Guild, 101 Fifth Ave., 10003.
French Book House, 796 Lexington Ave., 10021.
Librairie de France, 610 Fifth Ave., 10020.
R. H. Macy's Book Dept., Herald Square, 10001.
Stechert-Hafner, Inc., 31 E. 10th St., 10014.

Chicago, Ill.
Central Book Store, 119 N. Wabash, 60602.

Economy Book Store, 40 S. Clark St., 60603.
Kroch's & Brentano's, 29 S. Wabash, 60603.

San Francisco, Calif.
International Book Store, 1408 Market St., 94102.

Cincinnati, Ohio
Bertrand Smith's Acres of Books, 633 Main St., 45202.

Cambridge, Mass.
Schoenhof's Foreign Books, Inc., 1280 Massachu-
setts Ave., 02138.

The following publishers have an extensive list of
foreign language books and will supply their catalogs
upon request.

D. C. Heath and Co., 285 Columbus Ave., Boston,
Mass. 02116.
Henry Holt and Co., 383 Madison Ave., New York,
N.Y. 10017.
Appleton-Century-Crofts, Inc., 440 Park Ave. S.,
New York, N.Y. 10016.
Oxford University Press, 417 Fifth Ave., New York,
N.Y. 10016.
Prentice-Hall, Inc., U.S. Highway No. 9W, Engle-
wood Cliffs, N.J.
University of Chicago Press, 5750 Ellis Ave.,
Chicago, Ill. 60637.

French periodicals

France-Amérique, 1111 Lexington Ave., New York,
N.Y. 10021, is published weekly. The subscription
rate is $7.00 for one year. Single issue, $0.20.
Sélection du Reader's Digest. Reader's Digest, Pleasant-
ville, N.Y. 10570, publishes monthly a selection of its
articles translated into French. Single issue, $0.50;
subscription rate for one year, $2.97.

French radio programs

Radio broadcasts in French provide a variety of intonation, expression, and subject matter, and thus offer an excellent means of quickening your comprehension. With a good short-wave receiver of the usual home type you can hear French programs frequently during the day and evening. For detailed information on schedules, write to the following addresses. A postal card will usually suffice. Interesting and useful supplementary information will frequently be volunteered.

Voice of America, Foreign Language Division, 330 Independence Ave. S.W., Washington, D.C.

Canadian Broadcasting Corporation, International Service, P.O. Box 7000, Montreal, Canada.

The United Nations, Department of Public Information, United Nations Plaza, New York, N.Y.

North American Service, French Broadcasting System, 1290 Ave. of the Americas, New York, N.Y. 10019.

Swiss Shortwave Service, 28 Neuengasse, Berne, Switzerland.

CBF in Montreal on the regular band (690 kilocycles) is a French-language station. Its programs can be picked up in many cities of northern United States. For program schedules and information about other French-Canadian broadcasting stations, write to The Canadian Broadcasting Corporation, French Network, P.O. Box 6000, Montreal, P.Q., Canada.

For the latest information on broadcasts from a foreign country other than the countries mentioned above, write the embassy of that nation in Washington, D.C., or the consulate in New York City.

PRONUNCIATION

The simplified phonetic transcription is given as an aid to correct pronunciation. The transcription should be read as though it were English, with special attention to those sounds that have no English equivalents. The rules of French pronunciation are complex and not completely regular. Pages 14–17 give the nearest English equivalents, together with a few basic rules. **It is not necessary to memorize these rules** in order to benefit from the records. The best guide is listening to native speakers and attempting careful imitation.

In the phonetic system, accuracy is sometimes sacrificed for simplicity and ease of comprehension. You are urged to use it only as a temporary guide: abandon it as soon as possible. If you study French in a class or with a private teacher, the teacher may ask you to drop it so as to avoid confusion with other phonetic systems.

The nasal vowels

The nasal vowels, indicated in our transcription by a line over the letters, have the same values as the regular vowels except that they are pronounced "through the nose." Practice first by holding your nose, later by blocking the nasal passage from within, as when you have a cold.

an, am, em, en	a̅h̅n̅
in, im	e̅n̅
on, om	a̅w̅n̅
um, un	u̅h̅n̅

Silent final consonants

Generally speaking, when a word ends in a consonant the consonant is not pronounced. The most

SCHEME OF PRONUNCIATION

Letters	Our Transcription	Example	Notes on correct pronunciation
a	a	as in *ask*, *aunt*	
a	ah	as in *father*	
ai	e or eh	as in *met*	
au	oh	as in *notify*	See note on *o*.
b	b	as in *boy*	
c	k	as in *kite*	*c* is pronounced like *k* when it comes before *a*, *o*, or *u*. Before *e* and *i*, it is soft, like *s*.
c	s	as in *sit*	
ç	s	as in *sit*	*ç* is always pronounced like *s*.
ch	sh	as in *share*	
d	d	as in *day*	
e, è, ê	e or eh	as in *met*	
é	ay	as in *daytime*	This is a pure vowel, not a diphthong as in English. It is a shorter sound pronounced with the mouth more open.
e, eu, œu	uh	as in the *boy*	No exact equivalent in English. Round

the lips as if to say *oh*, but say *eh*. If you say *girl, err, demur, purr* without pronouncing the *r* (as is done in England and in some parts of eastern U.S.) you will give a good approximation. (The same sound occurs in German *können*, where it is short, and *Goethe*, where it is long.)

f	f	as in *f*are
g	g, gh	as in *g*o
g	zh	as in a*z*ure	*g* is hard before *a, o,* and *u*; soft before *e* and *i*.
gn	ny	as in ca*ny*on
h	—		Always silent.
i	ee	as in m*ee*t
j	zh	as in a*z*ure
k	k	as in *k*ite
l	l	as in *l*et
m	m	as in *m*et
n	n	as in *n*ote
o	aw	as in t*aw*dry	A shorter sound than in English.

Letters	Our Transcription	Example	Notes on correct pronunciation
o	oh	as in notify	This is a pure vowel, not a diphthong as in English. Practice by prolonging the sound of *oh* without permitting yourself to end on *oo*.
oi	wa	as in *wa*nt	
ou	oo	as in f*oo*d	
p	p	as in *p*et	
ph	f	as in *f*ell	
q	k	as in *k*ite	
r	r	as in *r*ed	May be rolled with the tip of the tongue as in Italian or Spanish. The Parisian *r*, which resembles the sound of gargling, is produced by vibration of the back of the tongue against the soft palate at the back of the mouth.
s	s or ss	as in *s*et	
s	z	as in *z*eal	Pronounced *s* at the beginning of a word or when doubled. A single *s* between two vowels is pronounced like *z*.

t	t	as in *tell*	
th	t	as in *ten*	Never pronounced like the *th* in English *this* or *thin*.
u	ew	as in *few*	There is no exact equivalent in English. The sound is properly made by rounding the lips as if to say *oo*, but saying *ee*. Practice by first saying *oo*, and WITHOUT CHANGING THE POSITION OF THE LIPS, say *ee*. (This sound is the same as the German *ü*, as in *müde*.)
v	v	as in *vase*	
w	v or w	as in *vase* or *went*	
x	ks	as in *picks*	
y	ee	as in *meet*	
z	z	as in *zone*	

common exceptions are *c*, *r*, *f*, and *l*, which are pronounced at the ends of words. You may remember these by thinking of the word CaReFuL.

Liaison

A usually-silent final consonant is often pronounced, however, when the following word begins with a vowel. In such case, the two words are tied together in pronunciation. For example: the *s* in *des* is ordinarily silent, but *des olives* is pronounced *day zaw-leev*.

The rules for liaison are complex and the usage is not regular. Listen carefully to the record and take note of the word groups that are habitually joined in this manner.

Accent

Pronounce each syllable distinctly, with a slight accent on the last syllable of each word or closely-related group of words. When the final syllable ends with a mute (unaccented) *e*, the stress is shifted to the next-to-last syllable. This shift is noted in the phonetic transcription by capitalizing the next-to-last syllable. For example, *possible* is transcribed as paw-SEE-bluh.

GREETINGS, INTRODUCTIONS AND SOCIAL CONVERSATION

1. **Good morning.**
Bonjour.
bawn-zhoor.

2. **Good evening.**
Bonsoir.
bawn-swahr.

3. **Hello.**
Bonjour.
bawn-zhoor.

4. **Good-bye.**
Au revoir.
awr-vwahr.

5. **I'll be seeing you.**
À bientôt.
ah byen-toh.

6. **My name is Charles.**
Je m'appelle Charles.
zhuh ma-pel shahrl.

7. **I wish to make an appointment with Mr. Desportes.**
Je désire prendre rendez-vous avec Monsieur Desportes.
zhuh day-zeer PRAHN-druh rahn-day-voo a-vek muh-syuh day-pawrt.

8. **May I introduce Mr. (Mrs., Miss) Simon?**
Puis-je vous présenter Monsieur (Madame, Mademoiselle) Simon?
PWEE-zhuh voo pray-zahn-tay muh-syuh (ma-dahm, mad-mwah-zel) see-mawn?

9. —— **My wife.**
Ma femme.
ma fahm.

10. —— **My husband.**
M<u>on</u> mari.
m<u>awn</u> ma-ree.

11. —— **My daughter.**
Ma fille.
ma FEE-uh.

12. —— **My son.**
M<u>on</u> fils.
m<u>awn</u> feess.

13. —— **My friend.**
M<u>on</u> ami.
maw na-mee.

14. —— **My sister.**
Ma sœur.
ma suhr.

15. —— **My brother.**
M<u>on</u> frère.
m<u>awn</u> frehr.

16. —— **My child.**
M<u>on</u> enfant.
maw n<u>ahn</u>-f<u>ahn</u>.

17. **The boy.**
Le garç<u>on</u>.
luh gar-s<u>awn</u>.

18. **The girl.**
La jeune fille.
la zhuhn FEE-yuh.

19. **The man.**
L'homme.
lawm.

20. The woman.
La femme.
la fahm.

21. I am glad to know you.
Je suis heureux de faire votre connaissance.
zhuh swee zuh-ruh duh fehr VAW-truh kawn-nes-sahnss.

22. I am here on a business trip.
Je suis ici en voyage d'affaires.
zhuh swee zee-see ahn vwah-yazh da-fehr.

23. —— On a vacation.
En vacances.
ahn va-kahnss.

24. We are traveling to Rouen.
Nous allons à Rouen.
noo zal-lawn zah roo-ahn.

25. I am a friend of Robert's.
Je suis un ami de Robert.
zhuh swee zuh na-mee duh raw-behr.

26. How are you?
Comment allez-vous?
kaw-mahn tal-lay-voo?

27. Fine, thanks.   And you?
Très bien, merci.   Et vous?
treh byen, mehr-see.   ay voo?

28. How are things?
Comment ça va?
kaw-mahn sa va?

29. All right.
Ça va.
sa va.

30. So, so.
Comme ci, comme ça.
kawm see, kawm sa.

31. How is your family?
Comment va votre famille?
kaw-mahn va VAW-truh fa-MEE-yuh?

32. Very well.
Très bien.
treh byen.

33. Please sit down.
Veuillez vous asseoir.
vuh-yay voo za-swahr.

34. I have enjoyed myself very much.
J'ai passé un moment très agréable.
zhay pa-say uhn maw-mahn treh za-gray-AH-bluh.

35. Give my regards to your aunt and uncle.
Mes amitiés à votre tante et à votre oncle.
may za-mee-tyay ah VAW-truh tahnt ay ah vaw TRAWN-kluh.

36. Come to see us.
Venez nous voir.
vuh-nay noo vwahr.

37. Give me your address and telephone number.
Donnez-moi votre adresse et votre numéro de
    téléphone.
*daw-nay-mwah vaw-tra-dress ay VAW-truh new-may-roh
    duh tay-lay-fawn.*

38. May I call on you again?
Puis-je revenir vous voir?
PWEE-zhuh ruh-vuh-neer voo vwahr?

39. I like you very much.
Vous m'êtes très sympathique.
voo met treh sen-pa-teek.

MAKING YOURSELF UNDER-STOOD

40. Do you speak English?
Parlez-vous anglais?
par-lay-voo ahn-gleh?

41. Does anyone here speak English?
Y a-t-il quelqu'un ici qui parle anglais?
ee a-teel kel-kuhn ee-see kee par lahn-gleh?

42. I speak only English.
Je ne parle que l'anglais.
zhuh nuh parl kuh lahn-gleh.

43. I speak a little French.
Je parle un peu français.
zhuh parl uhn puh frahn-seh.

44. Please speak more slowly.
Veuillez parler plus lentement.
vuh-yay par-lay plew lahnt-mahn.

45. I (do not) understand.
Je (ne) comprends (pas).
zhuh (nuh) kawn-prahn (pah).

46. Do you understand me?
Me comprenez-vous?
muh kawn-pruh-nay-voo?

47. Repeat it, please.
Veuillez répéter, s'il vous plaît.
vuh-yay ray-pay-tay, seel voo pleh.

48. Write it down, please.
Écrivez-le, s'il vous plaît.
ay-kree-vay-luh, seel voo pleh.

49. What does this mean?
Que veut dire ceci?
kuh vuh deer suh-see?

50. What is that?
Qu'est-ce que c'est que ça?
kes-kuh seh kuh sa?

51. How do you say "pencil" in French?
Comment dit-on "pencil" en français?
kaw-mahn dee-tawn "pencil" ahn frahn-seh?

52. How do you spell "Chateaubriand"?
Comment épelez-vous "Chateaubriand"?
kaw-mahn tay-play-voo "sha-toh-bree-ahn"?

USEFUL WORDS AND EXPRESSIONS

53. Yes.
Oui.
wee.

54. No.
Non.
nawn.

55. Perhaps.
Peut-être.
puh-TEH-truh.

56. Please.
S'il vous plaît.
seel voo pleh.

57. Excuse me.
Pardon.
par-dawn.

58. Thanks (very much).
Merci (beaucoup).
mehr-see (boh-koo).

59. You are welcome.
De rien.
duh ree-en.

60. I am a United States citizen.
Je suis Américain.
zhuh swee za-may-ree-ken.

61. My (mailing) address is 20 Park Street.
Mon adresse (pour le courrier) est rue du Parc, numéro vingt.
maw na-dress (poor luh koor-yay) eh rew dew park, new-may-roh ven.

62. What do you wish?
Que désirez-vous?
kuh day-zee-ray-voo?

63. Come here.
Venez ici.
vuh-nay zee-see.

64. Come in.
Entrez.
ahn-tray.

65. Wait a moment.
Attendez un moment.
at-tahn-day zuhn maw-mahn.

66. I am in a hurry.
Je suis pressé.
zhuh swee pres-say.

67. I am warm, cold.
J'ai chaud, froid.
zhay shoh, frwah.

68. I am hungry, thirsty.
J'ai faim, soif.
zhay fen, swahf.

69. I am busy, tired.
Je suis occupé, fatigué.
zhuh swee zaw-kew-pay, fa-tee-gay.

70. I am glad.
J'en suis content.
zhahn swee kawn-tahn.

71. I am sorry.
Je regrette.
zhuh ruh-gret.

72. What is the matter here?
Qu'y a-t-il?
kee a-teel?

73. It is all right.
C'est bien.
seh byen.

74. I (do not) know.
Je (ne) sais (pas).
zhuh (nuh) say (pah).

75. I (do not) think so.
Je (ne) le crois (pas).
zhuh (nuh) luh krwah (pah).

76. It doesn't matter.
Ça ne fait rien.
sa nuh feh ree-en.

77. How much is it?
Combien est-ce?
kawn-byen ess?

78. That is all.
C'est tout.
seh too.

79. Can you help me (tell me)?
Pouvez-vous m'aider (me dire)?
poo-vay-voo may-day (muh deer)?

80. Where is the washroom?
Où sont les lavabos?
oo sawn lay la-va-boh?

81. The men's room.
Messieurs.
may-syuh.

82. The ladies' room.
Dames.
dahm.

83. I am looking for my hotel.
Je cherche mon hôtel.
zhuh shehrsh maw no-tel.

84. I should like to walk there.
Je voudrais y aller à pied.
zhuh voo-dreh zee al-lay ah pyay.

85. Why?
Pourquoi?
poor-kwah?

86. When?
Quand?
kahn?

87. Who?
Qui?
kee?

88. What?
Quoi?
kwah?

89. How?
Comment?
kaw-mahn?

90. How long?
Combien de temps?
kawn-byen duh tahn?

91. How far?
À quelle distance?
ah kel deess-tahns?

92. Here.
Ici.
ee-see.

93. There.
Là.
la.

94. To.
À.
ah.

95. From.
De.
duh.

96. With.
Avec.
a-vek.

97. Without.
Sans.
sahn.

98. In.
Dans.
dahn.

99. On.
Sur.
sewr.

100. Near.
Près de.
preh duh.

101. Far.
Loin de.
lwen duh.

102. In front of.
Devant.
duh-vahn.

103. Behind.
Derrière.
deh-ryehr.

104. Beside.
À côté de.
ah koh-tay duh.

105. Inside
À l'intérieur.
ah len-tay-ryuhr.

106. Outside.
À l'extérieur.
ah lex-tay-ryuhr.

107. Empty.
Vide.
veed.

108. Full.
Plein.
plen.

109. Something.
Quelque chose.
kel-kuh shohz.

110. Nothing.
Rien.
ree-en.

111. Several.
Plusieurs.
plew-zyuhr.

112. Few.
Quelques.
kel-kuh.

113. (Much) more.
(Beaucoup) plus.
(boh-koo) plewss.

114. Less.
Moins.
mwen.

115. (A little) more.
(Un peu) plus.
(uhn puh) plewss.

116. Enough.
Assez.
as-say.

117. Too much.
Trop.
troh.

118. Many.
Beaucoup.
boh-koo.

119. Good.
Bon.
bawn.

120. Better (than).
Meilleur (que).
may-yuhr (kuh).

121. Best.
Le meilleur.
luh may-yuhr.

122. Bad.
Mauvais.
moh-veh.

123. Worse (than).
Pire (que).
peer (kᵥh).

124. Now.
Maintenant.
m͞ent-n͞ahn.

125. Immediately.
Tout de suite.
toot sweet.

126. Soon.
Bientôt.
by͞en-toh.

127. Later.
Plus tard.
plew tahr.

128. As soon as possible.
Le plus tôt possible.
luh plew toh paw-SEE-bluh.

129. It is (too) late.
Il est (trop) tard.
eel eh (troh) tahr.

130. It is early.
Il est tôt.
eel eh toh.

131. Slowly.
Lentement.
l͞ahnt-m͞ahn.

132. Slower.
Plus lentement.
plew l͞ahnt-m͞ahn.

133. Quickly.
Vite.
veet.

134. Faster.
Plus vite.
plew veet.

135. Look out!
Attention!
ah-tahn-syawn.

136. Listen.
Écoutez.
ay-koo-tay.

137. Look here.
Regardez.
ruh-gar-day.

DIFFICULTIES

138. I cannot find my hotel address.
Je ne peux pas trouver l'adresse de mon hôtel.
zhuh nuh puh pah troo-vay la-dress duh maw no-tel.

139. I have lost my friends.
J'ai perdu mes amis.
zhay pehr-dew may za-mee.

140. I left my purse, wallet in the hotel.
J'ai laissé mon sac, mon portefeuille à l'hôtel.
zhay les-say mawn sahk, mawn pawrt-FUH-yuh ah lo-tel.

141. I forgot my money, keys.
J'ai oublié mon argent, mes clés.
zhay oo-blee-ay maw nar-zhahn, may klay.

142. I have missed my train.
J'ai manqué mon train.
zhay mahn-kay mawn tren.

143. What am I to do?
Que dois-je faire?
kuh DWAH-zhuh fehr?

144. My glasses are broken.
Mes lunettes sont cassées.
may lew-net sawn kas-say.

145. Where can they be repaired?
Où peut-on les faire réparer?
oo puh-tawn lay fehr ray-pa-ray?

146. A hearing aid.
Un appareil acoustique.
uh nap-pa-ray a-kooss-teek.

147. The lost and found desk.
Le bureau des objets trouvés.
luh bew-roh day zawb-zheh troo-vay.

148. The American consulate.
Le consulat des États-Unis.
luh kawn-sew-la day zay-ta-zew-nee.

149. The police station.
Le commissariat de police.
luh kaw-mee-sa-rya duh paw-leess.

150. I will call a policeman.
Je vais appeler un agent.
zhuh vay za-play uh na-zhahn.

CUSTOMS AND BAGGAGE

151. Where is the customs?
Où est la douane?
oo eh la doo-an?

152. Here is my baggage, five pieces.
Voici mes bagages, cinq pièces.
vwah-see may ba-gazh, sen pyess.

153. —— My passport.
Mon passeport.
mawn pass-pawr.

154. —— My identification papers.
Mes papiers d'identité.
may pa-pyay dee-dahn-tee-tay.

155. —— My health certificate.
Mon certificat de santé.
mawn sehr-tee-fee-ka duh sahn-tay.

156. The bags on your left (right) are mine.
Les valises à votre gauche (droite) m'appartien-
nent.
lay va-leez zah VAW-truh gohsh (drwaht) ma-par-tyen.

157. I have nothing to declare.
Je n'ai rien à déclarer.
zhuh nay ree-eh nah day-kla-ray.

158. All this is for my personal use.
Tout ceci est pour mon usage personnel.
too suh-see eh poor maw new-zazh pehr-saw-nel.

159. Must I open everything?
Dois-je tout ouvrir?
DWAH-zhuh too too-vreer?

160. I cannot open that.
Je ne peux pas l'ouvrir.
zhuh nuh puh pas loo-vreer.

161. There is nothing here but clothing.
Il n'y a rien ici que des vêtements.
eel nee a ree-en ee-see kuh day vet-mahn.

162. These are gifts.
Ce sont des cadeaux.
suh sawn day ka-doh.

163. Are these things dutiable?
Ces objets sont-ils passibles de droits de douane?
say zawb-zheh sawn-teel pa-SEE-bluh duh drwah duh doo-an?

164. How much must I pay?
Combien dois-je payer?
kawn-byen DWAH-zhuh peh-yay?

165. This is all I have.
C'est tout ce que j'ai.
seh too skuh zhay.

166. Have you finished?
Avez-vous fini?
a-vay-voo fee-nee?

167. I cannot find my baggage.
Je ne peux pas trouver mes bagages.
zhuh nuh puh pah troo-vay may ba-gazh.

168. Where is the baggage checked?
Où enregistre-t-on les bagages?
oo ahn-ruh-ZHEE-struh-tawn lay ba-gazh?

169. The baggage room.
La salle des bagages.
la sal day ba-gazh.

170. The check room.
La consigne.
la kawn-SEEN-yuh.

171. The baggage check.
Le billet des bagages.
luh bee-yeh day ba-gazh.

172. I want to leave these bags for a while.
Je désire laisser ces valises en consigne.
zhuh day-zeer les-say say va-leez ahn kawn-SEEN-yuh.

172A. Do I pay now or later?
Dois-je payer maintenant ou plus tard?
DWAH-zhuh pay-yay ment-nahn oo plew tar?

173. Handle this very carefully.
Faites attention à celle-ci.
fet za-tahn-syawn ah sel-see.

TRAVEL:
GENERAL EXPRESSIONS

174. I want to go to the airline office.
Je désire aller au bureau de la compagnie d'aviation.
zhuh day-zee ral-lay oh bew-roh duh la kawn-pan-yee da-vee-ah-syawn.

175. —— The airport.
L'aérodrome.
la-ay-raw-drohm.

176. —— The bus station.
La gare des autobus.
la gar day zaw-toh-bewss.

177. —— The dock.
Le quai.
luh kay.

178. —— The railroad station.
La gare.
la gar.

179. How long does it take to go to Chartres?
Combien de temps faut-il pour aller à Chartres?
kawn-byen duh tahn foh-teel poor al-lay ah SHAR-truh?

180. When will we arrive at Cherbourg?
Quand arriverons-nous à Cherbourg?
kahn ah-ree-vuh-rawn-noo ah shehr-boor?

181. Is this the direct way to Versailles?
Est-ce la route directe de Versailles?
ess la root dee-rekt duh vehr-SAH-yuh?

182. Please show me the way to the business section.
Pouvez-vous m'indiquer le chemin du quartier des affaires, s'il vous plaît?
poo-vay-voo men-dee-kay luh shuh-men dew kar-tyay day za-fehr, seel voo pleh?

183. —— To the residential section.
Du quartier résidentiel.
dew kar-tyay ray-zee-dahn-syel.

184. —— To the shopping section.
Du quartier des magasins.
dew kar-tyay day ma-ga-zen.

185. —— To the city.
De la ville.
duh la veel.

186. —— To the village.
Du village.
dew veel-lazh.

187. Where do I turn?
Où dois-je tourner?
oo DWAH-zhuh toor-nay?

188. —— **To the north.**
Au nord.
oh nawr.

189. —— **To the south.**
Au sud.
oh sewd.

190. —— **To the west.**
À l'ouest.
ah lwest.

191. —— **To the east.**
À l'est.
ah lest.

192. —— **To the right.**
À droite.
ah drwaht.

193. —— **To the left.**
À gauche.
ah gohsh.

194. —— **At the traffic light.**
À la lumière.
ah la lewm-yehr.

195. **Where is it?**
Où est-ce?
oo ess?

196. **Is it on this side of the street?**
Est-ce de ce côté-ci de la rue?
ess duh suh koh-tay-see duh la rew?

197. —— **On the other side of the street?**
De l'autre côté de la rue?
duh LOH-truh koh-tay duh la rew?

198. —— **Across the street?**
En face?
en fass?

199. —— At the corner?
Au coin de la rue?
oh kwen duh la rew?

200. —— In the middle?
Au·milieu?
oh meel-yuh?

201. —— Straight ahead.
Tout droit.
too drwah.

202. —— Forward.
En avant.
ah na-vahn.

203. —— Back.
En arrière.
ah na-ree-ehr.

204. Am I going in the right direction?
Est-ce la bonne direction?
ess la bawn dee-rek-syawn?

205. What street is this?
Quelle est cette rue?
keh leh set rew?

206. The circle.
Le rond-point.
luh rawn-pwen.

207. The place.
La place.
la plass.

208. The avenue.
L'avenue.
la-vuh-new.

TICKETS

209. Where is the ticket office?
Où est le guichet?
oo eh luh ghee-sheh?

210. How much is a ticket to Marseilles?
Combien coûte un billet pour Marseille?
kawn-byen koot uhn bee-yeh poor mar-SAY-yuh?

211. One-way ticket.
Un billet d'aller.
uhn bee-yeh dal-lay.

212. Round trip.
D'aller et retour.
dal-lay ay ruh-toor.

213. First class.
Première classe.
pruh-myehr klass.

214. Second class.
Seconde classe.
suh-gawnd klass.

215. Third class.
Troisième classe.
trwah-zyem klass.

216. Local.
L'omnibus.
lawm-nee-bews.

217. Express.
Le rapide.
luh ra-peed.

218. A reserved seat.
Une place réservée.
ewn plass ray-zehr-vay.

219. Can I go by way of Lyons?
Puis-je y aller en passant par Lyon?
pwee-zhee al-lay ahn pa-sahn par lee-awn?

220. May I stop on the way?
Puis-je m'arrêter en route?
PWEE-zhuh ma-reh-tay ahn root?

221. Can I get something to eat on the way?
Peut-on obtenir de quoi manger en route?
puh-taw nawp-tuh-neer duh kwah mahn-zhay ahn root?

BOAT

222. Can I go by boat to London?
Puis-je aller à Londres par bateau?
pwee-zha-lay ah LAWN-druh par ba-toh?

223. When does the next boat leave?
Quand part le prochain bateau?
kahn par luh praw-shen ba-toh?

224. When must I go on board?
À quelle heure dois-je m'embarquer?
ah keh luhr DWAH-zhuh mahn-bar-kay?

225. Can I land at le Havre?
Pourrai-je débarquer au Havre?
poor-RAY-zhuh day-bar-kay oh AH-vruh?

226. The captain.
Le capitaine.
luh ka-pee-ten.

227. The purser.
Le commissaire.
luh kaw-mee-sehr.

228. The steward.
Le garçon.
luh gar-sawn.

229. The deck.
Le pont.
luh pawn.

230. The deck chair.
La chaise de pont.
la shez duh pawn.

231. The cabin.
La cabine.
la ka-been.

232. The cabin steward.
Le garçon de cabine.
luh gar-sawn duh ka-been.

233. The lifeboat.
Le canot de sauvetage.
luh ka-noh duh sohv-tazh.

234. The life preserver.
La ceinture de sauvetage.
la sen-tewr duh sohv-tazh.

235. Dramamine.
De la dramamine.
duh la dra-ma-meen.

236. I am seasick.
J'ai le mal de mer.
zhay luh mal duh mehr.

AIRPLANE

237. Is there a bus service to the airport?
Y a-t-il un service d'autobus pour l'aéroport?
ee a-tee luhn sehr-veess daw-toh-bewss poor la-ay-raw-pawr?

238. At what time will they come for me?
À quelle heure viendra-t-on me chercher?
ah keh luhr vyen-dra-tawn muh shehr-shay?

239. When is there a plane to Rome?
À quelle heure y a-t-il un départ pour Rome?
ah keh luhr ee a-teel uhn day-par poor rawm?

240. Is food served on the plane?
Peut-on obtenir de quoi manger à bord?
puh-taw nawp-tuh-neer duh kwah mahn-zhay ah bawr?

241. How many kilos may I take?
Combien de kilos de bagages puis-je emporter?
kawn-byen duh kee-loh duh ba-gazh PWEE-zhuh ahn-pawr-tay?

242. How much per kilogram for excess?
Combien par kilo pour l'excédent?
kawn-byen par kee-loh poor lek-say-dahn?

TAXI

243. Please call a taxi for me.
Veuillez m'appeler un taxi.
vuh-yay map-lay uhn tak-see.

244. How far is it?
À quelle distance est-ce?
ah kel dees-tahnss ess?

245. How much will it cost?
Quel sera le prix?
kel suh-ra luh pree?

246. What do you charge per hour (kilometer)?
Combien prenez-vous de l'heure (du kilomètre)?
kawn-byen pruh-nay-voo duh luhr (dew kee-law-MEH-truh)?

247. Please drive more slowly (carefully).
Veuillez conduire plus lentement (prudemment).
vuh-yay kawn-dweer plew lahnt-mahn (prew-da-mahn).

248. Stop here.
Arrêtez ici.
ar-reh-tay zee-see.

249. Wait for me.
Attendez-moi.
at-tahn-day-mwah.

TRAIN

250. Where is the railroad station?
Où est la gare?
oo eh la gar?

251. When does the train for Lyons leave?
À quelle heure part le train pour Lyon?
ah keh luhr par luh tren poor lee-awn?

252. The boat train.
Le train-paquebot.
luh tren-pak-boh.

253. Where does the train leave?
D'où part le train?
doo par luh tren?

254. Please open the window.
Voulez-vous bien ouvrir la fenêtre?
voo-lay-voo byen oo-vreer la fuh-NEH-truh?

255. Close the window.
Fermez la fenêtre.
fehr-may la fuh-NEH-truh.

256. Where is the diner?
Où est le wagon-restaurant?
oo eh luh va-gawn-ress-taw-rahn?

257. May I smoke?
Puis-je fumer?
PWEE-zhuh few-may?

BUS, STREETCAR, AND SUBWAY

258. What bus do I take to Montmartre?
Quel autobus dois-je prendre pour aller à Mont-martre?
keh law-toh-bewss DWAH-zhuh PRAHN-druh poor al-lay ah mawn-MAR-truh?

259. The bus stop.
L'arrêt d'autobus.
lar-reh daw-toh-bewss.

260. The driver.
Le conducteur.
luh kawn-dewk-tuhr.

261. A transfer.
Une correspondance.
ewn kaw-ress-pawn-dahns.

262. Where does the subway for l'Étoile stop?
Où s'arrête le métro pour l'Étoile?
oo sar-ret luh may-troh poor lay-twahl?

263. Do you go near the Champs Elysées?
Passez-vous près des Champs-Elysées?
pas-say-voo preh day shahn-zay-lee-zay?

264. Do I have to change?
Dois-je changer?
DWAH-zhuh shahn-zhay?

265. Please tell me where to get off.
Veuillez me dire où il faut descendre.
vuh-yay muh deer oo eel foh day-SAHN-druh.

266. Off next stop, please.
Le prochain arrêt, s'il vous plaît.
luh praw-shen ar-reh, seel voo pleh.

AUTOMOBILE TRAVEL

267. Where can we rent a car?
Où pouvons-nous louer une automobile?
oo poo-vawn-noo loo-ay ew naw-toh-maw-beel?

268. I have an international driver's license.
J'ai un permis international.
zhay uhn pehr-mee en-tehr-na-syaw-nal.

269. Can you recommend a good mechanic?
Pouvez-vous m'indiquer un bon mécanicien?
poo-vay-voo men-dee-kay uhn bawn may-ka-nee-syen?

270. —— A gas station.
Un poste d'essence.
uhn pawst des-sahnss.

271. —— A garage.
Un garage.
uhn ga-razh.

272. Is the road good?
La route est-elle bonne?
la root eh-tel bawn?

273. Where does that road go?
Où va cette route?
oo va set root?

274. What town is this?
Comment s'appelle cette ville?
kawn-mahn sa-pel set veel?

275. The next one?
La prochaine?
la praw-shen?

276. Can you draw me a map?
Pouvez-vous me dessiner un plan?
poo-vay-voo muh des-see-nay uhn plahn?

277. How much is gas a liter?
Combien le litre d'essence?
kawn-byen luh LEE-truh des-sahnss?

278. Give me ten liters.
Donnez-moi dix litres.
daw-nay-mwah dee LEE-truh.

279. Please change the oil.
Veuillez changer l'huile.
vuh-yay shahn-zhay lweel.

280. Put water in the battery.
Mettez de l'eau dans les accus.
met-tay duh loh dahn lay za-kew.

281. Will you lubricate the car?
Voulez-vous bien graisser la voiture?
voo-lay-voo byen gres-say la vwah-tewr?

282. Adjust the brakes.
Ajustez les freins.
ah-zhew-stay lay fren.

283. Will you check the tires?
Voulez-vous bien regarder les pneus?
voo-lay-voo byen ruh-gar-day lay pnuh?

284. Can you fix the flat tire?
Pouvez-vous réparer le pneu crevé?
poo-vay-voo ray-pa-ray luh pnuh kruh-vay?

285. —— A puncture.
Une crevaison.
ewn kruh-vay-zawn.

286. —— A slow leak.
Une légère fuite.
ewn lay-zhehr fweet.

287. The engine overheats.
Le moteur chauffe.
luh maw-tuhr shohf.

288. The engine misses (stalls).
Le moteur rate (cale).
luh maw-tuhr raht (kal).

289. May I park here for a while?
Puis-je stationner ici un instant?
PWEE-zhuh sta-syaw-nay ee-see uh nen-stahn?

PARTS OF THE CAR

290. Accelerator.
L'accélérateur.
lak-say-lay-ra-tuhr.

291. Battery.
Les accus.
lay-za-kew.

292. Brake.
Le frein.
luh frēn.

293. Clutch.
L'embrayage.
lāhn-bray-azh.

294. Engine.
Le moteur.
luh maw-tuhr.

295. Gear shift.
Le changement de vitesse.
luh shāhnzh-māhn duh vee-tess.

296. Headlight.
Le phare.
luh far.

297. Horn.
Le klaxon.
luh klak-sāwn.

298. Spring.
Le ressort.
luh ruh-sawr.

299. Starter.
Le démarreur.
luh day-mar-ruhr.

300. Spare tire.
Le pneu de rechange.
luh pnuh duh ruh-shāhnzh.

301. Steering wheel.
Le volant.
luh vaw-lāhn.

302. Wheel.
La roue.
la roo.

AT THE HOTEL

303. I am looking for a good hotel.
Je cherche un bon hôtel.
zhuh shehrsh uhn baw noh-tel.

304. —— An inexpensive hotel.
Un hôtel à prix modérés.
uh noh-tel ah pree maw-day-ray.

305. —— A boarding house.
Une pension.
ewn pahn-syawn.

306. —— A furnished apartment.
Un appartement meublé.
uh nap-par-tuh-mahn muh-blay.

307. I (do not) want to be at the center of town.
Je (ne) veux (pas) être au centre de la ville.
zhuh (nuh) vuh (pah) ZEH-truh oh SAHN-truh duh la veel.

308. Where is it not noisy.
Où il n'y a pas de bruit.
oo eel nee a pah duh brwee.

309. I have a reservation for today.
J'ai réservé une chambre pour aujourd'hui.
zhay ray-zehr-vay ewn SHAHN-bruh poor oh-zhoord-wee.

310. Do you have a room, a vacancy?
Avez-vous une chambre, une vacance?
a-vay-voo zewn SHAHN-bruh, ewn va-kahnss?

311. —— An air-conditioned room.
Une chambre climatisée.
ewn SHAHN-bruh klee-ma-tee-zay.

312. —— A single room.
Une chambre à un lit.
ewn SHAHN-brah uhn lee.

313. —— A double room.
Une chambre pour deux personnes.
ewn SHAHN-bruh poor duh pehr-sawn.

314. —— With meals.
Avec repas.
a-vek ruh-pah.

315. —— Without meals.
Sans repas.
sahn ruh-pah.

316. —— With a double bed.
À un grand lit.
ah uhn grahn lee.

317. —— With bath.
Avec salle de bain.
a-vek sal duh ben.

318. —— With a shower.
Avec une douche.
a-vek ewn doosh.

319. —— With twin beds.
Avec lits jumeaux.
a-vek lee zhew-moh.

320. —— With a balcony.
Avec un balcon.
a-vek uhn bal-kawn.

321. —— A suite.
Un appartement.
uh nap-par-tuh-mahn.

322. —— **For tonight.**
Pour cette nuit.
poor set nwee.

323. —— **For three days.**
Pour trois jours.
poor trwah zhoor.

324. —— **For two persons.**
Pour deux personnes.
poor duh pehr-sawn.

325. What is the rate per day?
Quel est votre prix par jour?
keh leh VAW-truh pree par zhoor?

326. Are tax and room service included?
Est-ce que les taxes et le service sont compris?
ess-kuh lay tax ay luh sehr-veess sawn kawn-pree?

327. I should like to see the room.
Je voudrais bien voir la chambre.
zhuh voo-dreh byen vwahr la SHAHN-bruh.

328. I do not like this one.
Je n'aime pas celle-ci.
zhuh nem pah sel-see.

329. Upstairs.
En haut.
ahn oh.

330. Downstairs.
En bas.
ahn bah.

331. Is there an elevator?
Y a-t-il un ascenseur?
ee a-tee luh na-sahn-suhr?

332. Will you send for my bags?
Voulez-vous bien envoyer chercher mes bagages?
voo-lay-voo byen ahn-vwah-yay shehr-shay may ba-gazh?

333. Room service, please.
Le service, s'il vous plaît.
luh sehr-veess, seel voo pleh.

334. Please send a porter to my room.
Faites monter un porteur dans ma chambre, s'il
vous plaît.
*fet mawn-tay uhn pawr-tuhr dahn ma SHAHN-bruh,
seel voo pleh.*

335. —— A chambermaid.
Une femme de chambre.
ewn fahm duh SHAHN-bruh.

336. —— A bellhop.
Un chasseur.
uhn shas-suhr.

337. Please call me at nine o'clock.
Veuillez m'appeler à neuf heures.
vuh-yay map-lay ah nuh vuhr.

338. I want breakfast in my room.
Je désire avoir le petit déjeuner dans ma chambre.
*zhuh day-zeer a-vwahr luh puh-tee day-zhuh-nay dahn
ma SHAHN-bruh.*

339. Come back later.
Revenez plus tard.
ruh-vuh-nay plew tar.

340. Change the sheets today.
Changez les draps aujourd'hui.
shahn-zhay lay drah oh-zhoord-wee.

341. Bring me another blanket.
Apportez-moi encore une couverture.
ap-pawr-tay-mwah ahn-kawr ewn koo-vehr-tewr.

342. A pillow.
Un oreiller.
uh naw-ray-yay.

343. A pillowcase.
Une taie d'oreiller.
ewn tay daw-ray-yay.

344. Hangers.
Des cintres.
day SEN-truh.

345. Soap.
Le savon.
luh sa-vawn.

346. Towels.
Les serviettes.
lay sehr-vee-et.

347. A bath mat.
Un tapis de bain.
uhn ta-pee duh ben.

348. The bathtub.
La baignoire.
la ben-wahr.

349. The sink.
Le lavabo.
luh la-va-boh.

350. Toilet paper.
Le papier hygiénique.
luh pap-yay ee-zhee-ay-neek.

351. I should like to speak to the manager.
Je voudrais bien parler au gérant.
zhuh voo-dreh byen par-lay oh zhay-rahn.

352. My room key, please.
Ma clé, s'il vous plaît?
ma klay, seel voo pleh.

353. Have I any letters or messages?
Y a-t-il des lettres ou des messages pour moi?
ee a-teel day LEH-truh oo day mes-sazh poor mwah?

354. What is my room number?
Quel est le numéro de ma chambre?
keh leh luh new-may-roh duh ma SHAHN-bruh?

355. I am leaving at ten o'clock.
Je pars à dix heures.
zhuh par ah dee zuhr.

356. Please make out my bill.
Veuillez préparer ma note.
vuh-yay pray-pa-ray ma nawt.

357. Will you accept a check?
Voulez-vous bien accepter un chèque?
voo-lay-voo byen ak-sep-tay uhn shek?

358. Please forward my mail to American Express in Rome.
Veuillez faire suivre mon courrier à l'American Express à Rome.
vuh-yay fehr SWEE-vruh mawn koor-yay ah l'American Express a rawm.

359. May I store baggage here until tomorrow?
Puis-je vous laisser des bagages jusqu'à demain?
PWEE-zhuh voo les-say day ba-gazh zhews-kah duh men?

AT THE CAFE

360. The bartender.
Le barman.
luh bar-mahn.

361. A cocktail.
Un cocktail.
uhn kawk-tayl.

362. A drink.
Une boisson.
ewn bwah-sawn.

363. A fruit drink.
Un jus de fruit.
uhn zhew duh frwee.

364. A soft drink.
Une boisson gazeuse.
ewn bwah-sawn ga-zuhz.

365. A bottle of mineral water.
Une bouteille d'eau minérale.
ewn boo-tay doh mee-nay-ral.

366. A glass of port.
Un verre de porto.
uhn vehr duh pawr-toh.

367. Some beer (light, dark).
De la bière (blonde, brune).
duh la byehr (blawnd, brewn).

368. Some whiskey (and soda).
Du whiskey (avec du soda).
dew wees-kee (a-vek dew saw-da).

369. Some cognac.
Du cognac.
dew koh-nyak.

370. Some wine (red, white).
Du vin (rouge, blanc).
dew ven (roozh, blahn).

371. Some champagne.
Du champagne.
dew shahn-PAN-yuh.

372. A liqueur.
Une liqueur.
ewn lee-kuhr.

373. Let's have another.
Prenons-en un autre.
pruh-nawn zahn uh NOH-truh.

374. To your health!
À votre santé!
ah VAW-truh sahn-tay!

AT THE RESTAURANT

375. Where is there a good restaurant?
Où peut-on trouver un bon restaurant?
oo puh-tawn troo-vay uhn bawn ress-taw-rahn?

376. Breakfast.
Le petit déjeuner.
luh puh-tee day-zhuh-nay.

377. Lunch.
Le déjeuner.
luh day-zhuh-nay.

378. Dinner.
Le dîner.
luh dee-nay.

379. Supper.
Le souper.
luh soo-pay.

380. A sandwich.
Un sandwich.
uhn sahnd-weetsh.

381. A snack.
Un casse-croûte.
uhn kass-kroot.

382. At what time is dinner served?
À quelle heure servez-vous le dîner?
ah keh luhr sehr-vay-voo luh dee-nay?

383. Can we lunch (dine) now?
Pouvons-nous déjeuner (dîner) maintenant?
poo-vawn-noo day-zhuh-nay (dee-nay) ment-nahn?

384. The waitress.
La serveuse.
la sehr-vuhz.

385. The waiter.
Le garçon.
luh gar-sawn.

386. The headwaiter.
Le maître d'hôtel.
luh MEH-truh doh-tel.

387. Waiter!
Garçon!
gar-sawn!

388. There are two of us.
Nous sommes deux.
noo sawm duh.

389. Give me a table near the window.
Donnez-moi une table près de la fenêtre.
daw-nay-mwah ewn TA-bluh preh duh la fuh-NEH-truh.

390. We want to dine à la carte.
Nous voulons dîner à la carte.
noo voo-lawn dee-nay ah la kart.

391. —— Table d'hôte.
À prix fixe.
ah pree feeks.

392. Please serve us quickly.
Servez-nous vite, s'il vous plaît.
sehr-vay-noo veet, seel voo pleh.

393. Bring me the menu.
Apportez-moi le menu.
ap-pawr-tay-mwah luh muh-new.

394. —— The wine list.
La carte des vins.
la kart day ven.

395. —— A fork.
Une fourchette.
ewn foor-shet.

396. —— A knife.
Un couteau.
uhn koo-toh.

397. —— A plate.
Une assiette.
ewn as-syet.

398. —— A teaspoon.
Une cuillère à café.
ewn kwee-yeh rah ka-fay.

399. —— A large spoon.
Une cuillère à soupe.
ewn kwee-yeh rah soop.

400. I want something simple.
Je désire quelque chose de simple.
zhuh day-zeer kel-kuh shohz duh SEN-pluh.

401. —— Not too spicy.
Pas trop épicé.
pah troh pay-pee-say.

402. I like the meat rare.
J'aime la viande saignante.
zhem la vee-ahnd sen-yahnt.

403. —— Well done.
Bien cuite.
byen kweet.

404. This is not clean.
Ce n'est pas propre.
suh neh pah PRAW-pruh.

405. Take it away, please.
Emportez cela, s'il vous plaît.
ahn-pawr-tay suh-la, seel voo pleh.

406. This is cold.
C'est froid.
seh frwah.

407. I did not order this.
Je n'ai pas commandé cela.
zhuh nay pah kaw-mahn-day suh-la.

408. May I change this for a salad?
Pouvez-vous remplacer cela par une salade?
poo-vay-voo rahn-pla-say suh-la par ewn sa-lad?

409. Ask the headwaiter to come here.
Priez le maître d'hôtel de venir.
pree-ay luh MEH-truh doh-tel duh vuh-neer.

410. The check, please.
L'addition, s'il vous plaît.
la-dee-syawn, seel voo pleh.

411. Is the tip included?
Le pourboire, est-il compris?
luh poor-bwahr, eh-teel kawn-pree?

412. Is the service charge included?
Le service, est-il compris?
luh sehr-veess, eh-teel kawn-pree?

413. There is a mistake in the bill.
Il y a une erreur dans l'addition.
eel ya ewn ehr-ruhr dahn la-dee-syawn.

414. What are these charges for?
Pourquoi ces suppléments?
poor-kwah say sew-play-mahn?

415. Keep the change.
Gardez la monnaie.
gar-day la maw-neh.

416. The food and service were excellent.
La cuisine et le service étaient excellents.
la kwee-zeen ay luh sehr-veess ay-teh tex-eh-lahn.

MENU

417. Drinking water.
L'eau potable.
loh paw-TA-bluh.

418. —— With ice.
Avec de la glace.
a-vek duh la glas.

419. —— Without ice.
Sans glace.
sahn glas.

420. The bread.
Le pain.
luh pen.

421. The butter.
Le beurre.
luh buhr.

422. The sugar.
Le sucre.
luh SEW-kruh.

423. The salt.
Le sel.
luh sel.

424. The pepper.
Le poivre.
luh PWAH-vruh.

425. The sauce.
La sauce.
la sohss.

426. The oil.
L'huile.
lweel.

427. The vinegar.
Le vinaigre.
luh vee-NEH-gruh.

428. The mustard.
La moutarde.
la moo-tard.

429. The garlic.
L'ail.
LAH-yuh.

BREAKFAST FOODS

430. May I have some fruit juice?
Puis-je avoir du jus de fruit?
PWEE-zhuh a-vwahr dew zhew duh frwee?

431. —— Some orange juice.
Du jus d'orange.
dew zhew daw-rahnzh.

432. —— Some tomato juice.
Du jus de tomate.
dew zhew duh taw-maht.

433. —— Some stewed prunes.
Des pruneaux cuits.
day prew-noh kwee.

434. —— Some cooked cereal.
Des céréales cuites.
day say-ray-al kweet.

435. —— Some toast and jam.
Du toast avec de la confiture.
dew tohst a-vek duh la kawn-fee-tewr.

436. —— Some rolls.
Des petits pains.
day puh-tee pen.

437. —— An omelet.
Une omelette.
ewn awm-let.

438. —— Some soft-boiled eggs.
Des œufs à la coque.
day zuh ah la kawk.

439. —— Some medium-boiled eggs.
Des œufs quatre minutes.
day zhuh KA-truh mee-newt.

440. —— Some hard-boiled eggs.
Des œufs durs.
day zuh dewr.

441. —— Some fried eggs.
Des œufs sur le plat.
day zuh sewr luh pla.

442. —— Some scrambled eggs.
Des œufs brouillés.
day zuh broo-yay.

443. —— Some bacon and eggs.
Des œufs avec du lard.
day zuh a-vek dew lar.

444. —— **Some ham and eggs.**
Des œufs au jambon.
day zuh oh zhahn-bawn.

445. —— **Some waffles.**
Des gaufres.
day GOH-fruh.

446. —— **Some pancakes and syrup.**
Des crêpes avec du sirop.
day krep a-vek dew see-roh.

SOUPS AND ENTRÉES

447. I want some chicken soup.
Je désire du potage au poulet.
zhuh day-zeer dew paw-tazh oh poo-leh.

448. —— **Some vegetable soup.**
Du potage aux légumes.
dew paw-tazh oh lay-gewm.

449. —— **Some roast chicken.**
Du poulet rôti.
dew poo-leh roh-tee.

450. —— **Some fried chicken.**
Du poulet frit.
dew poo-leh free.

451. —— **Some beef.**
Du bœuf.
dew buhf.

452. —— **Some duck.**
Du canard.
dew ka-nar.

453. —— **Some goose.**
De l'oie.
duh lwah.

454. —— **Some lamb.**
Du gigot.
dew zhee-goh.

455. —— **Some liver.**
Du foie.
dew fwah.

456. —— **Some lobster.**
Du homard.
dew aw-mar.

457. —— **Some pork.**
Du porc.
dew pawr.

458. —— **Some roast beef.**
Du rosbif.
dew raws-beef.

459. —— **Some sardines.**
Des sardines.
day sar-deen.

460. —— **Some sausage.**
De la saucisse.
duh la saw-seess.

461. —— **Some shrimps.**
Des crevettes.
day kruh-vet.

462. —— **Some steak.**
Du bifteck.
dew bif-tek.

463. —— **Some veal.**
Du veau.
dew voh.

VEGETABLES AND SALAD

464. I want some asparagus.
Je désire des asperges.
zhuh day-zeer day zas-pehrzh.

465. —— **Some beans.**
Des haricots.
day a-ri-koh.

466. —— **Some cabbage.**
Du chou.
dew shoo.

467. —— **Some carrots.**
Des carottes.
day ka-rawt.

468. —— **Some cauliflower.**
Du chou-fleur.
dew shoo-fluhr.

469. —— **Some celery and olives.**
Du céleri et des olives.
dew sayl-ree ay day zaw-leev.

470. —— **Some cucumber.**
Du concombre.
dew kawn-KAWN-bruh.

471. —— **Some lettuce.**
De la laitue.
duh la leh-tew.

472. —— **Some mushrooms.**
Des champignons.
day shahn-peen-yawn.

473. —— **Some onions.**
Des oignons.
day zawn-yawn.

474. —— **Some peas.**
Des petits pois.
day puh-tee pwah.

475. —— **Some peppers.**
Des poivrons.
day pwahv-rawn.

476. —— **Some boiled potatoes.**
Des pommes de terre bouillies.
day pawm duh tehr boo-yee.

477. —— **Some fried potatoes.**
Des pommes de terre frites.
day pawm duh tehr freet.

478. —— **Some mashed potatoes.**
De la purée de pommes de terre.
duh la pew-ray duh pawm duh tehr.

479. —— **Some rice.**
Du riz.
dew ree.

480. —— **Some spinach.**
Des épinards.
day zay-pee-nahr.

481. —— **Some tomatoes.**
Des tomates.
day taw-maht.

FRUITS

482. I want an apple.
Je désire une pomme.
zhuh day-zee rewn pawm.

483. —— **Some cherries.**
Des cerises.
day suh-reez.

484. —— **A grapefruit.**
Une pamplemousse.
ewn pahn-pluh-mooss.

485. —— **Some grapes.**
Du raisin.
dew ray-zen.

486. —— **Some lemon.**
    Du citron.
    dew see-trawn.

487. —— **Some melon.**
    Du melon.
    dew muh-lawn.

488. —— **Some nuts (walnuts).**
    Des noix.
    day nwah.

489. —— **An orange.**
    Une orange.
    ew naw-rahnzh.

490. —— **A peach.**
    Une pêche.
    ewn pesh.

491. —— **Some raspberries.**
    Des framboises.
    day frahn-bwahz.

492. —— **Some strawberries.**
    Des fraises.
    day frez.

BEVERAGES

493. —— **Some black coffee.**
    Du café noir.
    dew ka-fay nwahr.

494. —— **Coffee with cream.**
    Un café crème.
    uhn ka-fay krem.

495. —— **Some milk.**
    Du lait.
    dew leh.

496. —— **Some tea.**
Du thé.
dew tay.

497. —— **Some lemonade**
De la citronnade.
duh la see-traw-nad.

DESSERTS

498. May I have some cake?
Puis-je avoir du gâteau?
PWEE-zhah-vwahr dew gah-toh?

499. —— **Some cheese.**
Du fromage.
dew fraw-mazh.

500. —— **Some cookies.**
De petits gâteaux secs.
duh puh-tee gah-toh sek.

501. —— **Some crepes suzette.**
Des crêpes Suzette.
day krep sew-zet.

502. —— **Some custard.**
De la crème renversée.
duh la krem rahn-vehr-say.

503. —— **Some chocolate ice cream.**
De la glace au chocolat.
duh la glas oh shaw-kaw-la.

504. —— **Some vanilla ice cream.**
De la glace à la vanille.
duh la glas ah la va-NEE-yuh.

CHURCH

505. I would like to go to church.
Je voudrais aller à l'église.
zhuh voo-dreh zal-lay ah lay-gleez.

506. A Catholic church.
Une église catholique.
ewn ay-gleez ka-taw-leek.

507. A Protestant (Anglican) church.
Un temple protestant (anglican).
uhn TAHN-pluh praw-tes-tahn (ahn-glee-kahn).

508. A synagogue.
Une synagogue.
ewn see-na-gawg.

509. When is the service (mass)?
Quelle est l'heure de l'office (de la messe)?
keh leh luhr duh law-feess (duh la mess)?

510. Is there an English-speaking priest (rabbi, minister)?
Y a-t-il un prêtre (un rabbin, un pasteur) qui parle anglais?
ee a-tee luhn PREH-truh (uhn ra-ben, uhn pas-tuhr) kee par lahn-gleh?

SIGHTSEEING

511. I want a guide who speaks English.
Je désire un guide qui parle anglais.
zhuh day-zeer uhn gheed kee par lahn-gleh.

512. What is the charge per hour (day)?
Quel est le prix de l'heure (de la journée)?
keh leh luh pree duh luhr (duh la zhoor-nay)?

513. I am interested in painting.
Je m'intéresse à la peinture.
zhuh men-tay-ress ah la pen-tewr.

514. —— Sculpture.
La sculpture.
la skewl-tewr.

515. —— Architecture.
L'architecture.
lar-shee-tek-tewr.

516. I want to see the native arts and crafts.
Je souhaite voir les métiers du pays.
zhuh soo -et vwahr lay may-tyay dew pay-ee.

517. —— The castle.
Le château.
luh shah-toh.

518. —— The cathedral.
La cathédrale.
la ka-tay-dral.

519. —— The museum.
Le musée.
luh mew-zay.

520. When does it open, close?
À quelle heure est l'ouverture, la fermeture?
a keh luhr eh loo-vehr-tewr, la fehrm-tewr?

521. Where is the entrance, exit?
Où est l'entrée, la sortie?
oo eh lahn-tray, la sawr-tee?

522. What is the price of admission?
Quel est le prix d'entrée?
keh leh luh pree dahn-tray?

AMUSEMENTS

523. I should like to go to a concert.
Je voudrais aller à un concert.
zhuh voo-dreh zal-lay ah uhn kawn-sehr.

524. —— To the movies.
Au cinéma.
oh see-nay-ma.

525. —— To a night club.
Dans une boîte de nuit.
dahn zewn bwaht duh nwee.

526. —— To the opera.
À l'opéra.
ah loh-pay-ra.

527. —— To the theater.
Au théâtre.
oh tay-AH-truh.

528. At the box office.
Au bureau de location.
oh bew-roh duh law-ka-syawn.

529. Is there a matinee today?
Y a-t-il matinée aujourd'hui?
ee a-teel ma-tee-nay oh-zhourd-wee?

530. When does the evening performance, the floorshow start?
À quelle heure commence la soirée, le spectacle?
ah keh luhr kaw-mahns la swah-ray, luh spek-TA-kluh?

531. Have you any seats for tonight?
Avez-vous des places pour ce soir?
ah-vay-voo day plass poor suh swahr?

532. An orchestra seat.
Un fauteuil d'orchestre.
uhn foh-TUH-yuh dawr-KES-truh.

533. A reserved seat.
Une place réservée.
ewn plas ray-zehr-vay.

534. In the balcony.
Au balcon.
oh bal-kawn.

535. The box.
La loge.
la lawzh.

536. Can I see well from there?
Pourrai-je bien voir de cet endroit?
poo-RAY-zhuh byen vwahr duh set ahn-drwah?

537. Where can we go to dance?
Où pouvons-nous aller danser?
oo poo-vawn-noo al-lay dahn-say?

538. What is the cover charge?
Quel est le couvert?
keh leh luh koo-vehr?

539. —— The minimum (charge).
Le minimum.
luh mee-nee-mum.

540. May I have this dance?
Voulez-vous danser?
voo-lay-voo dahn-say?

SPORTS

541. The beach.
La plage.
la plazh.

542. Fishing.
La pêche.
la pesh.

543. Golf.
Le golf.
luh gawlf.

544. Horse racing.
Les courses.
lay koorss.

545. Skating.
Le patinage.
luh pa-tee-nazh.

546. Skiing.
Le ski.
luh skee.

547. Soccer.
Le football.
luh foot-bal.

548. Swimming.
La natation.
la na-ta-syawn.

549. Swimming pool.
La piscine.
la pee-seen.

550. Tennis.
Le tennis.
luh teh-neess.

BANK AND MONEY

551. Where is the nearest bank?
Où est la banque la plus proche?
oo eh la bahnk la plew prawsh?

552. At which window can I cash this?
À quel guichet puis-je toucher ceci?
ah kel ghee-sheh PWEE-zhuh too-shay suh-see?

553. Can you change this for me?
Pouvez-vous me changer ceci?
poo-vay-voo muh shahn-zhay suh-see?

554. Will you cash a check?
Voulez-vous payer un chèque?
voo-lay-voo pay-yay uhn shek?

555. Do not give me large bills.
Ne me donnez pas de gros billets.
nuh muh daw-nay pah duh groh bee-yeh.

556. May I have some change?
Puis-je avoir de la petite monnaie?
pwee-zha-vwahr duh la puh-teet maw-neh?

557. I have traveler's checks.
J'ai des chèques de voyageur.
zhay day shek duh vwah-ya-zhuhr.

558. A letter of credit.
Une lettre de crédit.
ewn LEH-truh duh kray-dee.

559. A bank draft.
Une lettre de change.
ewn LEH-truh duh shahnzh.

560. What is the exchange rate on the dollar?
Quel est le cours du change?
keh leh luh koor dew shahnzh?

561. May I have twenty dollars' worth of French money?
Puis-je avoir vingt dollars en argent français?
pwee-zhah-vwahr ven daw-lahr ah nar-zhant frahn-seh?

USEFUL SHOPPING INFORM-ATION

562. I want to go shopping.
Je veux courir les magasins.
zhuh vuh koo-reer lay ma-ga-zen.

563. I like that.
J'aime cela.
zhem suh-la.

564. How much is it?
Combien est-ce?
kawn-byen ess?

565. It is very expensive.
C'est très cher.
seh treh shehr.

566. I prefer something better (cheaper).
Je préfère quelque chose de mieux (de moins cher).
zhuh pray-fehr kel-kuh-shohz duh myuh (duh mwen shehr).

567. Show me some others.
Montrez-m'en d'autres.
mawn-tray-mahn DOH-truh.

568. May I try this on?
Puis-je l'essayer?
PWEE-zhuh leh-say-yay?

569. Can I order one?
Puis-je en commander un?
pwee-zhahn kaw-mahn-day uhn?

570. How long will it take?
Combien de temps cela prendra-t-il?
kawn-byen duh tahn suh-la prahn-drah-teel?

571. Please take my measurements.
Veuillez prendre mes mesures.
vuh-yay PRAHN-druh may muh-zewr.

572. Can you ship it to New York?
Pouvez-vous l'expédier à New-York?
poo-vay-voo lex-pay-dyay ah New York?

573. Whom do I pay?
À qui dois-je payer?
ah kee DWAH-zhuh peh-yay?

574. Please bill me.
Veuillez m'envoyer la facture.
vuh-yay mahn-vwah-yay la fak-tewr.

MEASUREMENTS

575. What is the length?
Quelle est la longueur?
keh leh la lawn-guhr?

576. —— The width?
La largeur?
la lar-zhuhr?

577. —— The size?
La pointure?
la pwen-tewr?

578. How much is it per meter?
Combien le mètre?
kawn-byen luh MEH-truh?

579. It is ten meters long by four meters wide.
Il a dix mètres de long sur quatre mètres de large.
eel a dee MEH-truh duh lawn sewr KA-truh MEH-truh duh larzh.

580. High.
Haut.
oh.

581. Low.
Bas.
bah.

582. Large.
Grand.
grahn.

583. Small.
Petit.
puh-tee.

584. Medium.
Moyen.
mwah-yen.

585. Alike.
Semblable.
sahn-BLA-bluh.

586. Different.
Différent.
dee-fay-rahn.

587. A pair.
Une paire.
ewn pehr.

588. A dozen.
Une douzaine.
ewn doo-zen.

589. Half a dozen.
Une demi-douzaine.
ewn duh-mee-doo-zen.

COLORS

590. I want a lighter shade.
Je désire un ton plus clair.
zhuh day-zeer uhn tawn plew klehr.

591. —— A darker shade.
Un ton plus foncé.
uhn tawn plew fawn-say.

592. Black.
Noir.
nwahr.

593. Blue.
Bleu.
bluh.

594. Brown.
Brun.
bruhn.

595. Gray.
Gris.
gree.

596. Green.
Vert.
vehr.

597. Orange.
Orange.
aw-rahnzh.

598. Pink.
Rose.
rohz.

599. Purple.
Violet.
vyaw-leh.

600. Red.
Rouge.
roozh.

601. White.
Blanc.
blahn.

602. Yellow.
Jaune.
zhohn.

603. I want to buy a bathing cap.
Je veux acheter un bonnet de bain.
zhuh vuh zash-tay uhn baw-neh duh ben.

604. —— A bathing suit.
Un costume de bain.
uhn kawss-tewm duh ben.

605. —— A blouse.
Une blouse.
ewn blooz.

606. —— A brassiere.
Un soutien-gorge.
uhn soo-tyen-gawrzh.

607. —— A coat.
Un manteau.
uhn mahn-toh.

608. —— A dress.
Une robe.
ewn rawb.

609. —— Some children's dresses.
Des robes d'enfant.
day rawb dahn-fahn.

610. —— A pair of garters.
Une paire de jarretières.
ewn pehr duh zhar-tyehr.

611. —— **A pair of gloves.**
Une paire de gants.
ewn pehr duh g$\overline{ah}$n.

612. —— **A handbag.**
Un sac à main.
$\overline{uhn}$ sak ah m$\overline{en}$.

613. —— **Some handkerchiefs.**
Des mouchoirs.
day moo-shwahr.

614. —— **A hat.**
Un chapeau.
$\overline{uhn}$ sha-poh.

615. —— **A jacket.**
Une jaquette.
ewn zha-ket.

616. —— **Some lingerie.**
De la lingerie.
duh la l$\overline{en}$zh-ree.

617. —— **A nightgown.**
Une chemise de nuit.
ewn shuh-meez duh nwee.

618. —— **A raincoat.**
Un imperméable.
uh n$\overline{en}$-pehr-may-AH-bluh.

619. —— **A pair of shoes.**
Une paire de chaussures.
ewn pehr duh shoh-sewr.

620. —— **Some shoelaces.**
Des lacets.
day la-seh.

621. —— **A pair of slippers.**
Une paire de pantoufles.
ewn pehr duh p$\overline{ah}$n-TOO-fluh.

622. —— **A pair of socks.**
Une paire de chaussettes.
ewn pehr duh shoh-set.

623. —— **A pair of nylon stockings.**
Une paire de bas nylon.
ewn pehr duh bah nee-lawn.

624. —— **A suit.**
Un costume.
uhn kawss-tewm.

625. —— **A sweater.**
Un sweater.
uhn sweh-tuhr.

626. —— **Some ties.**
Des cravates.
day krah-vaht.

627. —— **Trousers.**
Un pantalon.
uhn pahn-ta-lawn.

628. —— **Some underwear.**
Des sous-vêtements.
day soo-vet-mahn.

629. Do you have some ash trays?
Avez-vous des cendriers?
a-vay-voo day sahn-dree-ay?

630. —— **A box of candy.**
Une boîte de bonbons.
ewn bwaht duh bawn-bawn.

631. —— **Some china.**
De la porcelaine.
duh la pawr-suh-len.

632. —— **Some dolls.**
Des poupées.
day poo-pay.

633. —— Some earrings.
Des boucles d'oreille.
day BOO-kluh daw-ray.

634. —— Some perfume.
Du parfum.
dew par-fuhn.

635. —— Some pictures.
Des tableaux.
day ta-bloh.

636. —— Some records.
Des disques.
day deesk.

637. —— Some silverware.
De l'argenterie.
duh lar-zhahn-tree.

638. —— Some toys.
Des jouets.
day zhoo-eh.

639. —— An umbrella.
Un parapluie.
uhn pa-ra-plwee.

640. —— A watch.
Une montre.
ewn MAWN-truh.

STORES

641. Where is the bakery?
Où est la boulangerie?
oo eh la boo-lahnzh-ree?

642. —— **The pastry shop.**
La pâtisserie.
la pah-teess-ree.

643. —— **A candy store.**
Une confiserie.
ewn kawn-feez-ree.

644. —— **A cigar store.**
Un bureau de tabac.
uhn bew-roh duh ta-bah.

645. —— **A clothing store.**
Un magasin d'habillement.
uhn ma-ga-zen dah-bee-yuh-mahn.

646. —— **A department store.**
Un grand magasin.
uhn grahn ma-ga-zen.

647. —— **A drug store.**
Une pharmacie.
ewn far-ma-see.

648. —— **A grocery.**
Une épicerie.
ewn ay-peess-ree.

649. —— **A hardware store.**
Une quincaillerie.
ewn ken-kah-yuh-ree.

650. —— **A hat shop.**
Une chapellerie.
ewn sha-pel-ree.

651. —— **A jewelry store.**
Une bijouterie.
ewn bee-zhoo-tree.

652. —— **A meat market.**
Une boucherie.
ewn boosh-ree.

653. —— **A shoemaker.**
Un cordonnier.
uhn kawr-daw-nyay.

654. —— **A shoe store.**
Un magasin de chaussures.
uhn ma-ga-zen duh shoh-sewr.

655. —— **A tailor shop.**
Un tailleur.
uhn ta-yuhr.

656. —— **A watchmaker.**
Un horloger.
uh nawr-law-zhay.

BOOKSTORE AND STATIONER'S

657. **Where is there a bookstore?**
Où se trouve une librairie?
oo suh troov ewn lee-bray-ree?

658. —— **A stationer's.**
Une papeterie.
ewn pap-tree.

659. —— **A news dealer.**
Un marchand de journaux.
uhn mar-shahn duh zhoor-noh.

660. **I want to buy a newspaper.**
Je désire acheter un journal.
zhuh day-zee rash-tay uhn zhoor-nal.

661. —— **A magazine.**
Une revue.
ewn ruh-vew.

662. —— **A dictionary.**
Un dictionnaire.
uhn deek-syaw-nayr.

663. —— **A guidebook.**
Un guide.
uhn gheed.

664. —— **A book.**
Un livre.
uhn LEE-vruh.

665. —— **A map of Paris.**
Un plan de Paris.
uhn plahn duh pa-ree.

666. I would like some postcards.
Je voudrais des cartes postales.
zhuh voo-dreh day kart paws-tal.

667. —— **Some writing paper.**
Du papier à lettre.
dew pap-yay ah LEH-truh.

668. —— **Some ink.**
De l'encre.
duh LAHN-kruh.

669. —— **A pencil.**
Un crayon.
uhn kreh-yawn.

670. —— **A fountain pen.**
Un stylo.
uhn stee-loh.

671. —— **Some envelopes (airmail).**
Des enveloppes (avion).
day zahn-vuh-lawp (a-vyawn).

672. —— **Some string.**
De la ficelle.
duh la fee-sel.

CIGAR STORE

673. Where is the nearest cigar store?
Où est le bureau de tabac le plus proche?
oo eh luh bew-roh duh ta-bah luh plew prawsh?

674. I want some cigars.
Je veux des cigares.
zhuh vuh day see-gar.

675. —— Some pipe tobacco.
Du tabac pour la pipe.
dew ta-bah poor la peep.

676. —— Some cigarette cases.
Des étuis à cigarettes.
day zay-twee ah see-ga-ret.

677. —— A lighter.
Un briquet.
uhn bree-keh.

678. —— A pack of American cigarettes.
Un paquet de cigarettes américaines.
uhn pa-keh duh see-ga-ret za-may-ree-ken.

679. Do you have a match?
Avez-vous une allumette?
a-vay-voo zewn al-lew-met?

PHOTOGRAPHY

680. I want a roll of (color) film.
Je désire un rouleau de pellicules (en couleurs).
zhuh day-zeer uhn roo-loh duh pel-lee-kewl (ahn koo-luhr).

681. Some movie film.

Des pellicules cinékodak.

day pel-lee-kewl see-nay-kaw-dak.

682. For this camera.

Pour cet appareil.

poor seh ta-pa-ray.

683. What is the charge for developing a roll?

Combien prenez-vous pour développer une bobine?

kawn-byen pruh-nay-voo poor dayv-law-pay ewn baw-been?

684. When will they be ready?

Quand seront-ils prêts?

kahn suh-rawn-teel preh?

DRUG STORE

685. Where is there a drug store where they understand English?

Où y a-t-il une pharmacie où l'on comprend l'anglais?

oo ee a-tee lewn far-ma-see oo lawn kawn-prahn lahn-gleh?

686. Can you fill this prescription?

Pouvez-vous remplir cette ordonnance?

poo-vay-voo rahn-pleer set awr-daw-nahns?

687. How long will it take?

Combien de temps vous faudra-t-il?

kawn-byen duh tahn voo foh-dra-teel?

688. I want some adhesive tape.

Je veux du sparadrap.

zhuh vuh dew spa-ra-drah.

689. —— Some alcohol.
De l'alcool.
duh lal-kawl.

690. —— An antiseptic.
Un antiseptique.
uh nahn-tee-sep-teek.

691. —— Some aspirin.
De l'aspirine.
duh las-pee-reen.

692. —— Some bobby pins.
Des épingles à cheveux.
day zay-PEN-gluh zah shuh-vuh.

693. —— Some cleaning fluid.
Un produit pour détacher.
uhn praw-dwee poor day-ta-shay.

694. —— Some cold cream.
Du cold-cream.
dew "cold cream."

695. —— A comb.
Un peigne.
uhn PEN-yuh.

696. —— Some corn pads.
Des toiles anticor.
day twahl ahn-tee-kawr.

697. —— Some cotton.
De l'ouate.
duh loo-wat.

698. —— A deodorant.
Un désodorisant.
uhn day-zaw-daw-ree-zahn.

699. —— An ice bag.
Un sac à glace.
uhn sak ah glas.

700. —— **Some iodine.**
De l'iode.
duh lee-awd.

701. —— **A mild laxative.**
Un laxatif doux.
uhn lax-ah-teef doo.

702. —— **Some lipstick.**
Du rouge à lèvres.
dew roozh ah LEH-vruh.

703. —— **Some safety pins.**
Des épingles de sûreté.
day zay-PEN-gluh duh sewr-tay.

704. —— **Some powder.**
Du talc.
dew talk.

705. —— **A razor.**
Un rasoir.
uhn ra-zwahr.

706. —— **Some razor blades.**
Des lames de rasoir.
day lam duh ra-zwahr.

707. —— **Some sanitary napkins.**
Des serviettes hygiéniques.
day sehr-vee-et zee-zhee-ay-neek.

708. —— **A sedative.**
Un calmant.
uhn kal-mahn.

709. —— **A bottle of shampoo.**
Un flacon de shampooing.
uhn fla-kawn duh shahn-pwen.

710. —— **A shaving lotion.**
Une lotion après la barbe.
ewn law-syawn a-preh la barb.

711. —— **Some shaving cream (brushless).**
De la crème à raser (à appliquer sans
blaireau).
*duh la krem ah rah-zay (ah ap-plee-kay sahn
blay-roh).*

712. —— **Some sun glasses.**
Des lunettes de soleil.
day lew-net duh saw-lay.

713. —— **Some suntan oil.**
De l'huile de soleil.
duh lweel duh saw-lay.

714. —— **A thermometer.**
Un thermomètre.
uhn tehr-maw-MEH-truh.

715. —— **(A tube of) toothpaste.**
(Un tube de) pâte dentifrice.
(uhn tewb duh) paht dahn-tee-freess.

716. —— **Some toothpowder.**
De la poudre dentifrice.
duh la POO-druh dahn-tee-freess.

LAUNDRY AND DRY CLEANING

717. Where is the nearest laundry?
Où est la blanchisserie la plus proche?
oo eh la blahn-sheess-ree la plew prawsh?

718. —— **The dry cleaner.**
La teinturerie.
la ten-tewr-ree.

719. Could I have some laundry done?
Puis-je faire laver des affaires?
PWEE-zhuh fehr la-vay day za-fehr?

720. To be washed, mended.
À faire laver, repriser.
ah fehr la-vay, ruh-pree-zay.

721. To be cleaned, pressed.
À faire nettoyer, repasser.
ah fehr neh-twah-yay, ruh-pas-say.

722. The belt is missing.
La ceinture manque.
la sen-tewr mahnk.

723. Can you sew on this button?
Pouvez-vous me coudre ce bouton?
poo-vay-voo muh KOO-druh suh boo-tawn?

724. —— The zipper.
La fermeture éclair.
la fehrm-tew ray-klehr.

BARBER SHOP AND BEAUTY PARLOR

725. Where is there a good barber?
Où se trouve un bon coiffeur?
oo suh troov uhn bawn kwah-fuhr?

726. A haircut, please.
Une coupe de cheveux, s'il vous plaît.
ewn koop duh shuh-vuh, seel voo pleh.

727. A shave, please.
Une barbe, s'il vous plaît.
ewn barb, seel voo pleh.

728. A shampoo.
Un shampoing.
uhn shahn-pwen.

729. A finger wave.
Une mise en plis.
ewn meez ahn plee.

730. A permanent.
Une permanente.
ewn pehr-ma-nahnt.

731. A facial.
Un massage facial.
uhn mas-sazh fa-syal.

732. A massage.
Un massage.
uhn mas-sazh.

733. A manicurist, please.
Une manucure, s'il vous plaît.
ewn ma-new-kewr, seel voo pleh.

734. I want a shoe shine.
Je veux faire cirer mes chaussures.
zhuh vuh fehr see-ray may shoh-sewr.

735. May I make an appointment for tomorrow?
Puis-je prendre rendez-vous pour demain?
PWEE-zhuh PRAHN-druh rahn-day-voo poor duh-men?

HEALTH AND ILLNESS

736. I wish to see an American doctor.
Je désire voir un docteur américain.
zhuh day-zeer vwahr uhn dawk-tuh ra-may-ree-ken.

737. I do not sleep well.
Je ne dors pas bien.
zhuh nuh dawr pah byen.

738. My head aches.
J'ai mal à la tête.
zhay mal ah la tet.

739. Must I stay in bed?
Dois-je rester au lit?
DWAH-zhuh res-tay oh lee?

740. May I get up?
Puis-je me lever?
PWEE-zhuh muh luh-vay?

741. I feel better.
Je me sens mieux.
zhuh muh sahn myuh.

DENTIST

742. Do you know a good dentist?
Connaissez-vous un bon dentiste?
kaw-nes-say-voo uhn bawn dahn-teest?

743. This tooth hurts.
Cette dent me fait mal.
set dahn muh feh mal.

744. Can you fix it (temporarily)?
Pouvez-vous l'arranger (provisoirement)?
poo-vay-voo lar-rahn-zhay (praw-vee-zwahr-mahn)?

745. I have lost a filling.
J'ai perdu un plombage.
zhay pehr-dew uhn plawn-bazh.

746. I do not want this tooth extracted.
Je ne veux pas faire arracher cette dent.
zhuh nuh vuh pah feh rar-ra-shay set dahn.

POST OFFICE

747. Where is the post office?
Où est la poste?
oo eh la pawst?

748. A letter to the U.S.A.
Une lettre pour les Etats-Unis.
ewn LEH-truh poor lay zay-tah-zew-nee.

749. How many stamps do I need?
A combien dois-je l'affranchir?
a kawn-byen DWAH-zhuh laf-rahn-sheer?

750. Three stamps of 15 francs denomination.
Trois timbres de quinze francs.
trwah TEN-bruh duh kenz frahn.

751. I want to send a money order.
Je désire envoyer un mandat-poste.
zhuh day-zee rahn-vwah-yay uhn mahn-da-pawst.

752. Give me a receipt, please.
Donnez-moi un récépissé, s'il vous plaît.
daw-nay-mwah uhn ray-say-pees-say, seel voo pleh.

753. By airmail.
Par avion.
pa rah-vyawn.

754. Parcel post.
Par colis postal.
par kaw-lee paws-tal.

COMMUNICATIONS: TELEPHONE

755. Where can I telephone.
Où puis-je téléphoner?
oo PWEE-zhuh tay-lay-faw-nay?

756. Will you telephone for me?
Voulez-vous bien téléphoner pour moi?
voo-lay-voo byen tay-lay-faw-nay poor mwah?

757. I want to make a local call, number ——.
Donnez-moi la ville, numéro ——.
daw-nay-mwah la veel, new-may-roh ——.

758. May I speak to Leon?
Puis-je parler à Léon?
PWEE-zhuh par-lay ah lay-awn?

TIME AND TIME EXPRESSIONS

759. What time is it?
Quelle heure est-il?
keh luh reh-teel?

760. It is two o'clock A.M., P.M.
Il est deux heures du matin, de l'après-midi.
eel eh duh zuhr dew ma-ten, duh la-preh-mee-dee.

761. It is half past three.
Il est trois heures et demie.
eel eh trwah zuhr ay duh-mee.

762. It is a quarter past four.
Il est quatre heures et quart.
eel eh kat ruhr ay kar.

763. It is a quarter to five.
Il est cinq heures moins le quart.
eel eh sen kuhr mwen luh kar.

764. At ten minutes to six.
À six heures moins dix.
ah see zuhr mwen deess.

765. At ten minutes past seven.
À sept heures dix.
ah seh tuhr deess.

DAYS OF THE WEEK

766. Monday.
Lundi.
luhn-dee.

767. Tuesday.
Mardi.
mar-dee.

768. Wednesday.
Mercredi.
mehr-kruh-dee.

769. Thursday.
Jeudi.
zhuh-dee.

770. Friday.
Vendredi.
vahn-druh-dee.

771. Saturday.
Samedi.
sam-dee.

772. Sunday.
Dimanche.
dee-mahnsh.

MONTHS AND SEASONS

773. January.
Janvier.
zhahn-vee-ay.

774. February.
Février.
fayv-ree-ay.

775. March.
Mars.
marss.

776. April.
Avril.
av-reel.

777. May.
Mai.
may.

778. June.
Juin.
zhwen.

779. July.
Juillet.
zhwee-yeh.

780. August.
Août.
oo.

781. September.
Septembre.
sep-TAHN-bruh.

782. October.
Octobre.
awk-TAW-bruh.

783. November.
Novembre.
naw-VAHN-bruh.

784. December.
Décembre.
day-SAHN-bruh.

785. Spring.
Le printemps.
luh pren-tahn.

786. Summer.
L'été.
lay-tay.

787. Autumn.
L'automne.
law-tawn.

788. Winter.
L'hiver.
lee-vehr.

789. NUMBERS.

One. Un. *ūhn.*

Two. Deux. *duh.*

Three. Trois. *trwah.*

Four. Quatre. *KA-truh.*

Five. Cinq. *sēnk.*

Six. Six. *seess.*

Seven. Sept. *set.*

Eight. Huit. *weet.*

Nine. Neuf. *nuhf.*

Ten. Dix. *deess.*

Eleven. Onze. *āwnz.*

Twelve. Douze. *dooz.*

Thirteen. Treize. *trez.*

Fourteen. Quatorze. *ka-tawrz.*

Fifteen. Quinze. *kēnz.*

Sixteen. Seize. *sez.*

Seventeen. Dix-sept. *dee-set.*

Eighteen. Dix-huit. *dee-zweet.*

Nineteen. Dix-neuf. *deez-nuhf.*

Twenty.　Vingt.　*vēn.*

Twenty-one.　Vingt et un.　*vēn-tay-ūhn.*

Twenty-two.　Vingt-deux.　*vēnt-duh.*

Thirty.　Trente.　*trahnt.*

Thirty-one.　Trente et un.　*trahn-tay-ūhn.*

Forty.　Quarante.　*ka-rahnt.*

Fifty.　Cinquante.　*sēn-kahnt.*

Sixty.　Soixante.　*swa-sahnt.*

Seventy.　Soixante-dix.　*swa-sahnt-deess.*

Seventy-one.　Soixante et onze.　*swa-sahn tay awnz.*

Eighty.　Quatre-vingts.　*ka-truh-vēn.*

Eighty-one.　Quatre-vingt-un.　*ka-truh-vēn-ūhn.*

Ninety.　Quatre-vingt-dix.　*ka-truh-vēn-deess.*

Ninety-one.　Quatre-vingt-onze.　*ka-truh-vēn-awnz.*

Ninety-two.　Quatre-vingt-douze.　*ka-truh-vēn-dooz.*

One hundred.　Cent.　*sahn.*

Two hundred.　Deux cents.　*duh sahn.*

One thousand.　Mille.　*meel.*

Two thousand.　Deux mille.　*duh meel.*

1956.　Mil neuf cent cinquante-six.　*meel nuh sahn sen-kahnt-seess.*

FRENCH FOOD
and
WINE SUPPLEMENT

FRENCH FOOD SUPPLEMENT

A visit to France can be your introduction to the imagination, spirit and tradition of the French cuisine. France is very rich in natural resources and all these resources have been used creatively. In less abundant regions, dishes are prepared using foods and ingredients that are relatively unknown and unpopular in this country. Ingredients are extensive, seasonings are subtle and regional resources are developed to the utmost. French dining is not only enhanced by the art of cooking but also by the complementary art of serving. There is a pride and joy in cooking and serving—whether it be of a simple or complex nature—that is at once noticeable. To understand the spirit and tradition of French cooking and dining is to begin to understand the spirit of the French people.

Breakfast in France is quite simple. It has come to be known as the continental breakfast; but in France more accurately *café complet* consists of freshly baked *croissants, brioches* or French bread served with butter and jelly and *café au lait*, that is, coffee with hot milk. Lunch, usually served between 12 and 2 o'clock, is frequently the main meal of the day. It is a leisurely meal and carefully planned. Dinner is customarily served between 7 and 9 o'clock and is as significant as the mid-day meal. Wines are, of course, served with all meals; whether it be an ordinary table wine or a carefully chosen vintage wine, drinking wine is considered a natural complement for the full enjoyment of food.

The list that follows is by no means complete but is meant to serve as an introduction to the tourist to what may at first appear to be a bewildering French menu. Dishes are alphabetized according to the French and usually appear as they would on a French menu. Descriptions are necessarily brief and have been written for the purposes of rapid reference.

Note on Hors D'Oeuvres

The preparation and serving of hors d'œuvres can be quite simple or very elaborate but it remains an essential part of the French cuisine. The custom of serving cold or hot hors d'œuvres for lunch and dinner is traditional on all French menus. Interesting and imaginative combinations of fish, shellfish, salads, eggs, vegetables, meats and marinated dishes are usually included and served in small tasteful combinations. We have not included a list of the extensive hors d'œuvres possible for the purpose of this "Native Food List." Listed simply as HORS D'ŒUVRES on the menu, this dish varies daily with the spirit of the chef, and the quality of the restaurant you choose to dine in. It is usually an adventure in the tradition of French dining.

A NOTE ON FRENCH WINES

France is renowned for producing a great variety of wines and for producing wines of good quality. Viticulture is an ancient and respected art in France and French wine growers are concerned with maintaining the quality of their product. The authenticity and quality of the wine is also guaranteed by the laws, known as *Appelation Contrôlée* or *Appelation d'Origine*, which regulate the entire process of wine production in most areas of the country. These laws ensure that the wine label accurately identifies the contents of the bottle.

The wine laws governing the production of wine in a specific vineyard are stricter than the laws controlling the production of wine in larger areas. Therefore, a wine label which indicates a specific vineyard of origin suggests a wine of a higher quality than a label which denotes only a region or district of origin. This is why the first-quality, famous French wines are always bottled under the name of a specific vineyard.

When you are traveling through France do not feel that you should drink only the great wines. Most of these wines are readily available in the United States whereas many delightful local wines are not. The local wines will be pleasant, inexpensive and unique and will add to the pleasures of dining in France.

"Wine rules" are the result of much loving experimentation by food and wine connoisseurs and are not meant to be social dictates. One should feel free to experiment, but the time-honored "rules" are often helpful.

An elementary rule-of-thumb concerning the serving of wine with food is that red wines complement red meats and white and rosé wines complement fish, shellfish, chicken and the lighter meats, such as veal. Champagne is considered an excellent dinner wine and goes well with almost any dish.

General Suggestions for Selecting Dinner Wines:

With	Try
Chicken Fish Shellfish Light meats (veal)	Dry white wine or rosé. Chablis is particularly good with oysters.
Red meats Game, cheese	Full-bodied red wines, i.e., Burgundy, Bordeaux or Rhône.
Turkey	Dry red or white wine.
Sweet dessert Fruit	Sweet white wine, i.e., Sauternes or Barsac. Extra dry champagne is also good.

WINE LIST

Apéritifs

It is customary in France to take a leisurely apéritif (an alcoholic wine drink), rather than a strong cocktail, to stimulate the appetite before the dinner. Popular apéritifs are:

Byrrh.
Medium dry, ruby red wine with body and subtle flavor.

Campari.
Very dry, rather bitter white wine from Italv.

Dubonnet. Rich red, slightly sweet wine.

Pernod.
Pale green liqueur with a distinctive anisette flavor. Served with water and ice.

Sherry.
Amber colored wine from Spain. Dry, light varieties are best served before dinner or with dinner.

Vermouth.
Red (sweet) or white (dry) wine interestingly flavored with aromatic herbs and bitters. Usually served on ice with a twist of lemon peel.

Vermouth-cassis.
Vermouth and cassis (a sirupy-liqueur made from black currants) in a pleasant tasting mixture with ice and vichy water.

Red and White Table Wines

Alsatian wines. White wines similar to Rhine wines, produced in three different types.

> **Riesling.** Dry white wine.

> **Traminer.**
> Medium dry wine with a pronounced spicy or fruity flavor and renowned bouquet.

> **Sylvaner.** Mild, pleasant white wine.

Barsac. Sweet, rich white wine of delicate aroma. Generally used as a dessert wine.

Bordeaux. Also referred to as claret.* Red wines comparable in quality to Burgundy, but drier and lighter with elegant bouquet and flavor. The following districts produce excellent claret:

> **Saint-Émilion.**
> Full-bodied and robust wines with strong bouquet.

* In the U.S.A.

Pomerol.
Somewhat lighter wines, but otherwise similar to Saint-Emilion.

Médoc.
Typical claret. Light-bodied, mellow with long lasting taste.

Burgundy. Full-bodied dry wine of excellent color, flavor and strong bouquet. Produced in both red and white varieties. Some popular and generally available Burgundies are:

Nuits-Saint-Georges.
Red, very full-bodied with remarkable bouquet.

Pommard.
Somewhat lighter and more delicate.

Beaujolais.
Fresh, light red Burgundy with an earthy bouquet. Excellent when drunk young.

Chablis.
Very dry, light white wine with a peculiar "steely" flavor.

Champagne. The best sparkling wine in the world, produced in white and pink varieties. Champagne is made in varying degrees of sweetness and types:

Brut. Very dry.

Extra Sec (Extra Dry). Semi-dry.

Sec. Less dry, actually rather sweet.

Blanc de blancs. Extremely light and effervescent.

Rhône. Full-bodied red wines of strong bouquet. Popular varieties are:

Côte-Rôtie.

Châteauneuf-du-Pape.

Rosé. Light, refreshing pink wines which are excellent when drunk young. The most popular rosé wines are:

Tavel. Dry, rather tart, highly praised wine.

Provence. Light, fresh and fruity wine.

Sauternes.   Sweet, rich white wine.   Generally used as a dessert wine.

Brandies, Liqueurs, Cordials

Brandies.

Armagnac.   Superior French brandy.

Calvados.   Very fine apple brandy.

Cognac.

The very best brandy in the world, originating from the district of Cognac.

Liqueurs and cordials. (Sweetened, flavored and sometimes artificially colored.)

Benedictine.

Amber-colored liqueur made with a variety of herbs and characterized by its delicacy.

Chartreuse.

Made with a cognac base and with a mixture of many aromatic herbs. There are green and yellow varieties of this unusual liqueur, the green containing more alcohol than the yellow.

Cointreau.

Colorless, rich liqueur of subtle orange flavor.

Crème de menthe.

Strongly peppermint flavored liqueur which is available in luminous green or colorless varieties.

Framboise.

Delicious, rich, colorless brandy made from distilled raspberries.

Grand Marnier.

Strongly orange-flavored liqueur made with a cognac base.

Mirabelle.

Alsatian brandy made from yellow plums.

Kirsch.   Dry, colorless brandy made from dark, sour cherries and characterized by a piquant, slightly bitter almond flavor.

Beers

Bière blonde.   Light beer or ale.

Bière brune.   Dark beer or stout.

Guide to Vintages

Recent good and great vintage years. Dates in italics indicate great years, whereas roman dates indicate exceptionally good years.

Alsatian wine: *1959*, 1958, 1957, 1955, *1953*

Red Burgundy: *1959*, 1958, 1957, 1955, 1953, 1952, 1949, *1947*, *1945*, 1934, *1929*

White Burgundy: *1959*, 1958, 1957, 1955, 1953, 1952, 1950, 1949, *1947*, 1945

Bordeaux (Claret): *1959*, 1958, 1957, 1955, 1953, 1952, 1949, *1947*, *1945*, 1934, *1929*

Rhône wines: *1959*, 1958, 1957, 1955, 1952, 1949, *1947*, *1945*

Champagne: 1959, 1958, 1957, 1955, 1953, 1952, 1949, *1947*

Sauternes and Barsac: *1959*, 1958, 1953, 1952, 1949, *1947*, *1945*, 1937, 1934, *1929*

Glossary of General Wine Terms

Vin blanc. White wine.

Vin borru.
Light young Burgundy often available in restaurants by the glass.

Vin doux. Sweet wine.

Vin fin. Fine wine.

Vin gris. Rosé wine of Alsace.

Vin jaune.
Yellowish-amber colored wine resembling a dry sherry in flavor and bouquet.

Vin mousseux. Sparkling wine.

Vin ordinaire. Ordinary table wine.

Vin de paille.
"Straw" wine, gray-pink in color. A sweet, rich dessert wine.

Vin du pays. Regional or local wine.

Vin rosé. Pink wine.

Vin rouge. Red wine.

Vin sec. Dry wine.

USEFUL MENU TERMS

L'addition.   The check.
À la carte OR **carte.**
A list of individual dishes, each at a fixed price.
À prix fix.   At a fixed price.
Carte du jour.   Menu or bill of fare.
Couvert.   Cover charge.
Déjeuner.   Luncheon.
Dîner.   Dinner.
Petit déjeuner.   Breakfast.
Inclusif.   Included.
Plat.   A single course or dish.
Selon grosseur OR **S.G.**   According to size.
Service compris.   Service charge included.
Sommelier.   Wine steward.
Spécialités.   Specialties.
Supplément.   Additional charge.
Sur commande.   On special order.
Table d'hôte.   Menu at a fixed price served "family style"

STYLES OF PREPARATION:
SOME GENERAL TERMS

À la . . .   In the style of . . .
À l'andalouse.
Served with green peppers and tomatoes.
À l'africaine.   Served with rice.
À l'anglaise.   Boiled.
À l'aubergiste.
Prepared in the customary style of the restaurant or inn.
À l'autrichienne.
Austrian style; seasoned with paprika and caraway seeds.
À la grecque.   Greek style with olive oil.
À la minute.   Quickly prepared.

À la mode de . . .   In the style of . . .

À la russe.   With sour cream.

À point.
Used to describe the preparation of meat as medium or done to a turn.

Assorti.   Assorted.

Au gratin.
Baked in a cream sauce with a garnish of cheese and bread crumbs.

Au jus.   With natural juice of the beef.

Au kirsch.   Mixed with the brandy, kirsch.   Usually refers to fresh fruit.

Au lait.   With milk.

Au maigre.   Meatless dish.

Au vin rouge.   Prepared with red wine.

Bellevue.
Served in aspic accompanied by a white sauce garnished with truffles, tongue and tarragon.

Bien cuit.   Well done.

Blanchi.   Blanched.

Bouilli.   Boiled.

Bourgeoisie.
Cooked in hearty family style with carrots, onions, potatoes and bacon.

Braisé.   Braised.

Brochette.
Meat or fish and vegetables grilled on a skewer over the open fire.

Brouillé.   Scrambled.

Canapé.
Small, daintily prepared open sandwich served as an appetizer.

Casserole.
Food served in an individual saucepan or dish.

Charolais.   Charcoal broiled.

Châtelaine.
Garnish of artichoke hearts, tomatoes and small roast potatoes.

Chiffonade.   Served with shredded vegetables.

Cocotte.   Served in an individual earthenware or copper pot.

Confiserie.   Sweets and candies.

Croûton.
Diced toast fried in butter or oil and used for soups, salads and garnish.

Désossé.   Boneless.

Diable.   Deviled. Prepared in highly seasoned style.

Dolmas.
Chopped liver or other meat and vegetables wrapped in vine leaves, cabbage leaves or peppers.

Émincé.   Minced meat dish served with a seasoned sauce.

En papillote.
Baked in an oiled paper bag to allow steaming in natural juices.

Entremets.   Small course served after the roast.

Escalope.   Thinly sliced meat.

Étuvé.   Stewed.

Farci.   Stuffed.

Flambé.   Served flaming in rum or brandy.

Frit.   Fried.

Galantine.
Rolled or pressed meat or poultry prepared with stock and gelatine and served cold. Usually a buffet or luncheon dish.

Gelé.   Jellied.

Glacé.   Iced.

Gratiné.   Served with bread crumbs or cheese.

Grillade.   A grilled dish.

Grillé.   Grilled or broiled.

Haché.   Chopped or sliced.

Hachis.   Hash.

Hongroise.
Hungarian style; prepared with sour cream and paprika.

Indienne. Curried.

Jardinière.
Fresh vegetables attractively cut and used as a garnish.

Julienne. Cut in thin strips.

Lyonnaise. Served with onions.

Macédoine. Combination of cut up fruits or vegetables.

Macéré. Pickled.

Nature OR **au naturel.** Plain, uncooked.

Panaché. Mixed.

Pané. Prepared with bread crumbs.

Parmentier. Prepared with potatoes.

Pâté.
Creamy paste made with fish, poultry or meat and distinctively seasoned.

Paysanne. Country style; a regional preparation.

Printanière.
Garnished with diced spring vegetables.

Provençale.
Prepared with oil, vinegar, herbs, garlic. Served hot or cold.

Purée. Mashed or strained.

Quenelle.
Oval shaped balls made with chopped chicken, veal or fish and seasonings.

Ragoût. Stew.

Rissoles OR **rissolettes.**
Minced meat fried in a thin pastry.

Rochambeau.
Garnish of carrots, lettuce and cauliflower.

Saignant. Rare.

Saumuré. Pickled or marinated.

Sauré. Cured in smoke.

Sauté.   Gently browned in butter.

Timbale.
Traditional French mould for baking and preparing hot or cold desserts.

Véronique.   Garnished with grapes.

Viande fumée.   Smoked meat.

SAUCES AND CONDIMENTS

Allemande.
White sauce made with veal stock, egg yolk, lemon juice and seasonings.

Anchois.   Anchovy sauce.

Aurore.   Chicken and tomato sauce.

Béarnaise.
Subtly seasoned sauce made with butter, shallots, egg yolks, tarragon and wine.

Béchamel.   Thick, creamy white sauce.

Bercy.
Sauce made with fish stock, wine and shallots.

Beurre blanc.   White butter sauce.

Beurre fondu.   Melted butter sauce.

Beurre noir.
Browned butter with vinegar and parsley.

Beurre roux.   Browned butter sauce.

Bigarrade.
Duck stock, orange and lemon juice and rind combined in a sauce for duckling.

Bolognaise.
Spicy sauce prepared with garlic, tomatoes, vegetables and seasonings.

Bonne femme.   Rich, creamy sauce.

Bordelaise.
Wine sauce made with stock, seasonings, shallots and wine.

Bourguignonne.
Wine sauce made with onions, spices, beef stock and red wine.

Bretonne.
Fish sauce made with fish stock, leek, celery, beans and mushrooms.

Câpre.
Caper sauce made with fish stock, butter and capers; served with fish.

Cardinal.   Béchamel sauce and red lobster butter.

Chasseur.
Butter or olive oil, mushrooms, tomato sauce, meat glaze combined with white wine and brandy.

Créole.
Sauce made with onions, tomatoes, peppers for rice.

Diable.
Hot, spicy sauce made with wine, vinegar, fresh pepper and shallots.

Duglère.
Rich creamy sauce made with fish stock, butter, eggs, cream, wine and tomatoes.

Espagnol.
Rich brown sauce made with meat stock, vegetables and tomatoes.

Fines herbes.
Sauce made with finely chopped herbs; usually served with fish, fowl, and omelettes.

Gastronome.   White wine sauce.

Génoise.
Cold sauce made with mayonnaise, cream and nuts.

Hollandaise.
Rich, creamy sauce made with egg yolks, butter and lemon juice, usually served with fish or vegetables.

Indienne.   Curry sauce.

Journeaux.   Chicken liver sauce.

Livornaise.   Sauce of anchovy paste, oil and eggs.

Madère.   Madeira wine sauce.

Maître d'hôtel.
Light sauce made with butter, lemon juice and parsley.

Marguery.   White wine sauce for fish and seafood.

Matelote.
Sauce of fish stock, wine, mushrooms and anchovies; usually served with fish.

Meunière.   Butter sauce.

Mornay.
Rich, cream sauce garnished with grated cheese.

Mousseline.   Creamy hollandaise sauce.

Moutarde.   Mustard.

Nantua.
Sauce made with crayfish, white wine, vegetables and tomatoes.

Newburg.
Rich sauce combining sherry, cream, egg yolks and lobster meat.

Niçoise.
Sauce made with onions, garlic, oil, tomatoes and vegetables used for fish, chicken or meat.

Normande.
Cream sauce combined with fish stock and mushrooms.

Périgueux.
Sauce made with stock, wine, tomatoes and truffles.

Périgourdine.
Rich madeira wine made with truffles and goose livers.

Piquante.   Spicy sauce.

Poivrade.
Highly seasoned sauce made with freshly ground peppercorns, onions and stock.

Portugaise.   Tomato, vegetable sauce.

Printanière.
White sauce with green vegetables and parsley.

Raifort.   Horseradish.

Ravigote.
Sauce made with wine, vinegar, stock, shallots and fresh tarragon; served hot or cold.

Régence.
White wine sauce with mushrooms and truffles.

Rouennaise.
Red wine sauce made with duck livers, bay leaves and thyme; usually served with duck.

Robert.
Spicy meat sauce made with onions, wine, meat stock or glaze, mustard and sugar.

Sabayan.
Rich frothy dessert sauce made with marsala wine, eggs, sugar whipped together and flavored to taste.

Saupiquet.   Spiced vinegar sauce.

Soubise.   Béchamel sauce with finely minced onions.

Smitane.
Sour cream sauce with sautéed onions and white wine.

Suprême.   Rich sweet cream sauce.

Tartare.
Cold, well-seasoned sauce made with mayonnaise, vinegar, mustard, pickles, herbs; usually served cold.

Verte.
Mayonnaise seasoned and colored with green vegetables.

Velouté.   Rich, creamy sauce for chicken or fish.

Vinaigrette.
Sauce or a dressing for vegetables or salads made with oil, vinegar, mustard and spices.

BREADS AND BUTTERS

Brioche.   Light, sweet, breakfast roll.

Croissant.   Flaky, crescent-shaped breakfast roll.

Pain.   Bread.

Pain doré.   French toast.

Pain grillé.   Toast.

Pain noir.   Wheat or rye bread.

Petit pain.   Roll.

Beurre.   Butter.

Beurre d'anchois.   Anchovy butter.

SOUPS

Bisque.
Rich, creamy soup made with a basic fish stock, fish or shellfish.

Bisque d'écrevisses.   Crayfish soup.

Bisque de homard.   Lobster soup.

Bisque d'huîtres.   Oyster soup.

Bouillabaisse.
Hearty fish soup much like stew made with a variety of fish, wine, tomatoes, onion, garlic, saffron, fennel and served with French bread.

Bouillabaisse à la marseillaise.
Bouillabaisse prepared with Mediterranean fish.

Bouillon.   Broth.

Consommé.
Clear broth made with chicken or meat and vegetables and served with various garnishes.

Consommé brunoise.   Clear beef soup.

Consommé vert.
Green consommé made with asparagus tips, peas, string beans, sorrel leaves and chervil.

Crème d'asperges.   Cream of asparagus soup.

Crème de carottes.   Cream of carrot soup.

Crème de champignons.   Cream of mushroom soup.

Crème d'épinards.   Cream of spinach soup.

Crème Olga.   Mushroom and onion soup.

Crème vichyssoise.
Cold, piquant soup made with potatoes and leek.

Marmite OR **petite marmite.**
Classic French soup prepared with beef, poultry, and vegetables. Traditionally served in an earthenware pot with toasted bread and cheese.

Potage.   Soup.

Potage à l'ail.   Garlic soup served with cheese.

Potage bonne femme.   Leek and potato soup.

Potage bourguignonne.
Hearty vegetable and meat soup.

Potage cressonière.
Purée of potato and watercress soup.

Potage grand duc.   Cauliflower soup.

Potage du jour.   Particular soup prepared for the day.

Potage au lentilles.   Lentil soup.

Potage Marguerite.   Kidney bean soup.

Potage à la milanaise.
Vegetable and meat soup with cheese.

Potage parmentier.   Potato soup.

Potage portugais.   Spicy, tomato soup.

Potage à la reine.   Cream of chicken soup.

Potage au vermicelle.   Noodle soup.

Potage de volaille.   Chicken broth.

Pot-au-feu.
Traditional hearty soup similar to petite marmite.

Poule au pot.   Chicken and broth served in the pot.

Soupe au chou.   Cabbage soup.

Soupe aux moules.   Mussel soup.

Soupe à l'oignon.
Onion soup served with toasted bread and cheese.

Soupe aux poissons.   Fish soup.

Vichyssoise.
Potato and leek soup made with milk or cream; served cold.

FISH AND SHELLFISH

Aigrefin.   Haddock.

Arachon.   French oyster.

Banquet.   Prawn.

Bar de mer.   Sea bass.

Blanchaille.   Whitebait.

Brème.   Bream.   (A fish in the carp family.)

Brochet badoise.
Baked pike prepared with sour cream.

Cabillaud au four.   Baked codfish.

Carpe à la polonaise.
Carp cooked in red wine with onions and almonds.

Carrelet.   Flounder.

Caviar frais.   Fresh caviar.

Chaudfroid de saumon.
Cold salmon in jellied sauce.

Clovisse.   Clam.

Coquillages.   Shellfish.

Coquilles provençale.
Scallops in a dried mushroom sauce.

Coquilles St.-Jacques.   Baked scallops au gratin.

Cotriade.   Fish stew.

Crevettes.   Shrimps.

Croustade aux langoustes.
Pastry shell filled with creamed lobster.

Darne.   Slice of fish with the bone.

Darne Montmorency.
Slice of salmon with mushrooms and olives.

Écrevisse.   Crayfish.

Escargots.   Snails.

Escargots à la bourguignonne.
Snails cooked in wine sauce and baked in well-seasoned butter.

Esturgeon.   Sturgeon.

Féra.   Whitefish.

Filet de sole amandine.
Fillet of sole sautéed in butter sauce and garnished with shredded almonds.

Filet de sole bonne femme.
Sole prepared in a white wine sauce and hollandaise sauce.

Filet de sole dieppoise.
Sole prepared in a sauce of mussels and shrimps.

Filet de sole aux huîtres.
Fillet of sole poached, sautéed in butter and prepared with oysters.

Filet de sole maconnaise.
Sole in red wine sauce.

Filet de sole à la Mornay.
Fillet of sole with a cheese sauce.

Flet. Flounder.

Flétan. Halibut.

Fruits de mer. Seafood.

Hareng. Herring.

Hareng fumé. Smoked herring.

Hareng mariné. Marinated herring.

Hareng salé. Kipper.

Hareng saur. Red herring.

Homard. Lobster.

Homard à l'américaine OR armoricaine.
Lobster meat in a rich tasty sauce of butter, stock, fresh tomatoes, wine and brandy.

Homard en bellevue OR aspic de homard en bellevue. Lobster in fish aspic.

Homard à la newburg.
Lobster newburg (lobster meat in a sherry cream sauce).

Homard Marguerite.
Lobster with mushrooms and truffles in a rich cream sauce with wine.

Homard parisienne.
Cold, boiled lobster served in the shell with mayonnaise dressing.

Homard thermidor.
Lobster thermidor. (Lobster meat mixed with rich cream sauce and wine. Baked in the shell, covered with cheese and bread crumbs.)

Huîtres en cheval.
Oysters on horseback. (Oysters rolled in bacon, grilled and served on toasted bread squares.)

Huîtres en coquille. Oysters on the half shell.

Laitance. Fish roe.

Langouste.
Crawfish OR crayfish. (European lobster similar to American varieties.)

Langoustines.
Prawns. (A large kind of shrimps.)

Loup. Bass.

Maquereau mariné. Marinated mackerel.

Marennes. Small oysters.

Matelote. Fish stew.

Médaillons de poissons. Halibut steaks.

Merlan. Whiting.

Merluche. Dried codfish.

Morue provençale. Codfish in tomato sauce.

Moules. Mussels.

Moules bordelaise. Mussels in wine sauce.

Moules farcies. Stuffed mussels.

Moules marinière.
Mussels steamed in a wine sauce with butter and shallots.

Moules panées. Baked mussels.

Moules à la provençale.
Mussels cooked in a spicy sauce made with oil, garlic, wine, fish stock and herbs.

Œufs de poisson. Fish roe.

Palourde. Clam.

Panchouse. Fish stew made with fresh-water fish.

Perche. Perch.

Pieuvre. Octopus.

Plie. Plaice. (Similar to sole.)

Pochouse bourguignonne. Fish stew.

Poireaux aux crevettes. Shrimps with leeks.

Poisson. Fish.

Poulpe. Octopus.

Quenelles de brochet. Fish or meat dumplings.

Raie au beurre noir.
Sea skate sautéed in brown butter.

Rouget au fenouil.
Mediterranean fish cooked in olive oil with bacon and seasoned with fennel.

Rousette. Variety of salmon.

Royan. Herring.

Salmis de poissons. Mixed seafood.

Sardines à l'huile. Sardines in olive oil.

Sardines à la niçoise.
Sardines cooked in a white wine sauce with mushrooms and spices.

Saumon fumé. Smoked salmon.

Saumon glacé OR **chaudefroid de saumon.**
Cold salmon in aspic.

Saumonneau. Baby salmon.

Scampi. Large shrimp prepared in seasoned garlic sauce.

Sole Albert. Sole with oysters and mushrooms.

Sole arlésienne.
Sole cooked with garlic, onions, tomatoes and spices.

Sole Colbert.
Boned fillet of sole, breaded and fried.

Sole gratin.
Sole baked with bread crumbs, mushrooms and cheese.

Sole limande. Lemon sole.

Sole Marguery.
Sole prepared with a rich, cream sauce of shrimps, mushrooms and wine.

Sole Mirabeau. Sole with anchovy sauce.

Sole Olga.
Sole poached and stuffed into baked potatoes and garnished with a rich shrimp sauce.

Sole Orly.
Sole fried in deep fat and served with a tomato sauce.

Sole vin blanc.
Sole in a cream sauce made with wine, stock, egg yolks and cream.

Tacaud. Variety of codfish.

Tanche. Variety of carp.

Thon à l'huile. Tuna fish in oil.

Truite. Trout.

Truite au bleu.
Fresh trout poached in water and vinegar resulting in a bluish color.

Truite saumonée.   Salmon trout.

Turbatin.   Native French fish similar to flounder.

Turbot.   Fish similar to flounder.

Turbot bonne femme.
Turbot cooked in cream sauce with wine, mushrooms and shallots.

Turbot au champagne.
Turbot poached in white wine or champagne.

Vandoise.   Variety of carp.

Vangeren.   Variety of carp.

ENTRÉES: MEATS AND MISCELLANEOUS DISHES

Bifteck tartare.
Raw chopped beef usually served with an accompanying sauce.

Blanquette d'agneau.
Lamb stew with mushrooms and onions.

Blanquette de veau.
Veal stew in a rich sauce.

Bœuf à la mode.
Marinated beef braised with carrots, mushrooms and onions.

Bœuf bouilli.   Boiled beef.

Bœuf bourguignonne.
Beef stew with red wine, tomato paste, onions and mushrooms.

Bœuf en daube.   Beef stew with red wine.

Bœuf salé.   Corned beef.

Carbonnade.
Beef prepared in the oven with onions, beer and beef stock.

Carbonnade à la flamande.
Browned slices of beef cooked in seasoned beer sauce.

Carré de porc rôti.   Roast loin of pork.

Cassoulet.
Native stew made with white beans, sausage, pork,
tomatoes (sauce or paste), onions, garlic and bacon
rind cooked and served in casserole.

Cervelles au beurre noir.
Calves' brains served with browned butter.

Cervelles beurre noisette.
Poached brains in hazel-butter sauce.

Châteaubriand.
Thick steak cut from middle of the beef fillet.

Choucroute garni.
Hot sauerkraut served with a variety of meats and
sausages.

Côte de veau.   Veal cutlet.

Côtelette de veau en papillote.
Veal cutlet baked and served in a sealed paper con-
tainer.

Côtes de bœuf.   Ribs of beef.

Côtes de porc.   Spareribs.

Couchon de lait.   Suckling pig.

Cuisseau.   Leg of veal.

Daube.
Stew usually made with lamb or mutton, herbs,
vegetables and wine.

Entrecôte.   Thin, rib steak.

Entrecôte chasseur.
Steak served with a wine sauce.

Entrecôte château.   Large, thick steak.

Entrecôte minute.
Very thin slice of beef steak for quick broiling.

Épaule de veau.   Shoulder of veal.

Escalopes de veau.   Thin slices of veal.

Escalopes de veau panées.
Thinly sliced veal, lightly breaded and fried and
garnished with lemon and chopped egg.

Escalopes de veau à la royale.
Sliced veal in brandied cream sauce.

Estouffade.
Braised beef with wine, stock, onions, garlic, herbs and mushrooms.

Estouffade de bœuf.
Beef stew with red wine and onions.

Estouffade aux haricots.
Stew of sausage, pork and white beans.

Filet de bœuf.
Fillet of beef; one of the choicest cuts.

Filet mignon.   Choice fillet of beef.

Filet de porc.   Pork fillet.

Filets de veau.   Veal fillets.

Foie à la bordelaise.
Liver with wine and mushrooms.

Foie gras.
Finely ground goose liver mixed with chicken force-meat, truffles, salt, pepper and brandy. Served hot or cold as a delicacy.

Foie à la provençale.
Liver sautéed in garlic butter.

Foie de veau.   Calf's liver.

Foie de veau moissonière.
Calf's liver with onions, herbs and red wine.

Foie de volaille.   Chicken liver.

Fricadelles.
Meat patties made with chopped beef, onions and seasoning.

Fricandeau.   Sliced meat in wine sauce.

Fricassée de veau.   Veal stew.

Gigot d'agneau.   Leg of lamb.

Gigot de mouton.   Leg of mutton.

Goulasch de veau.   Veal goulash.

Grenouilles sautées fines herbes.
Frog's legs sautéed in butter with finely chopped herbs and lemon.

Haricots de mouton.
Mutton stew with beans, onions and carrots.

Jambon.   Ham.

Jambon à la crème.   Ham in cream sauce.

Jambon au madère.
Ham in madeira wine sauce.

Langue de bœuf.   Ox tongue.

Langue de veau.   Calf's tongue.

Navarin de mouton.   Mutton stew.

Noisettes d'agneau.   Boneless lamb chops.

Paupiette.
Large slice of meat, rolled and stuffed with forcemeat
and baked.

Paupiette de veau.
Slice of veal, stuffed and rolled.

Petit salé.   Salt or pork bacon.

Pied de veau.   Calf's feet grilled or baked.

Plat de côtes au chou.
Boiled beef and cabbage.

Poitrine de veau.   Breast of veal.

Pot-au-feu.
Boiled beef with vegetables; served in the pot.

Potée limousine.
Stew of pork, cabbage and chestnuts.

Pré salé.
Lamb fed in salt marshes causing its distinctive
taste; a regional specialty of Normandy.

Quenelles.
Dumpling stuffed with a tasty preparation of minced
meat or fish.

Queue de bœuf.   Ox tail.

Quiche Lorraine.
Open-baked pie filled with a mixture of chopped ham
or bacon, beaten eggs, cream, cheese.

Ragoût d'agneau.   Lamb stew.

Ragoût de bœuf.   Beef stew.

Ragoût de mouton jardinière.
Mutton stew with finely cut carrots, turnips, onions,
potatoes and peas.

Ris d'agneau. Lamb sweetbreads.

Ris de veau. Veal sweetbreads.

Rognons de mouton. Sheep kidneys.

Rognons de veau. Veal kidneys.

Saucisse. Fresh pork sausage.

Saucisson. Smoked pork sausage.

Sauté de bœuf. Beef sautéed in a wine, tomato sauce.

Selle d'agneau. Saddle of lamb.

Selle de veau. Saddle of veal.

Steak à l'américaine.
Grilled steak served with a fried egg.

Steak de cheval. Horsemeat steak.

Steak Diane. Very thin steak.

Steak haché. Chopped steak.

Steak au poivre.
Choice cut of steak covered with freshly crushed peppercorns, melted butter and then broiled.

Tendrons de veau. Braised veal.

Terrine maison.
Finely ground mixture of chicken, goose liver, pork and distinctive seasonings; very often a regional specialty.

Tournedos.
Center cut of beef or a small thick fillet, sautéed or grilled and garnished in many different ways.

Tournedos à la béarnaise.
Grilled fillet of beef served with béarnaise sauce.

Tournedos chasseur.
Beef fillet cooked in butter and garnished with a sauce of mushrooms, tomatoes and wine.

Tournedos Rossini.
Grilled fillet of beef garnished with goose liver, truffles and a wine sauce.

Tranche de bœuf. Slice of steak.

Tripe à la mode.
Tripe cooked with tomatoes, shallots and apple brandy.

Veau.   Veal.

Veau Marengo.
Sliced veal sautéed in olive oil with wine, mushrooms,
tomatoes.

Veau mimosa.
Veal with port wine and fresh tarragon.

POULTRY AND GAME

Aguillettes de caneton.   Breast of duckling.

Ailerons de poulet.   Chicken wings.

Bécasse.   Woodcock.

Bécassine.   Snipe.

Brochettes de foies de volaille.
Skewer of chicken livers brushed with butter and grilled
on an open flame.

Cailles.   Quails.

Canard.   Duck.

Canard Montmorency.
Duck cooked in a rich sauce made with whole bing
cherries.

Canard aux olives.
Duck prepared in a sauce with olives.

Canard à la presse.
Pressed duck served in flaming brandy.

Canard sauvage.   Wild duck.

Caneton.   Duckling.

Caneton aux cerises.   Duckling with cherries.

Caneton à l'orange.
Duckling with orange sauce.

Caneton aux pommes.
Roast duckling with apples.

Caneton rouennais.
Duckling served with a rich sauce made with duck
stock, cognac, red wine and onions.

Caneton sauvage.   Wild duckling.

Civet de lièvre à la française.
Hare cooked in a red wine sauce with mushrooms and onions.

Civette. Hare stew.

Coq à la bourguignonne.
Rooster simmered with wine, brandy, salt pork, onions, mushrooms and a bouquet of herbs.

Coq au vin.
Chicken cooked in wine, brandy, onions and mushrooms.

Côtelettes de poulet. Chicken cutlets.

Cou d'oie farci. Stuffed goose neck.

Crêpes niçoises.
Pancake stuffed with a tasty chicken preparation.

Crochettes de volaille. Chicken croquettes.

Croustade de volaille.
Pastry shells filled with well-seasoned minced chicken.

Dinde. Turkey.

Dindonneau. Young turkey.

Faisan. Pheasant.

Filets de poulets. Breasts of chicken.

Foies de volaille et rognons au vin rouge.
Chicken livers and kidneys sautéed in red wine.

Fricassée de poulet. Chicken fricassee.

Galantine de volaille.
Chicken served in a decorative mould; made with chicken stock and gelatin.

Ganga. Species of grouse.

Gelinotte. Hazel hen (a game bird).

Grand coq de bruyère. Grouse.

Grive. Thrush.

Lapereau. Young rabbit.

Lapin. Rabbit.

Lapin chasseur.
Rabbit stew with wine, tomatoes, mushrooms and herbs.

Lièvre. Hare.

Lièvre à la royale.
Hare stew made with wine, vinegar, carrots, onions and garlic.

Marcassin.   Young boar.

Merles.   Blackbirds; usually roasted.

Oie OR **oison.**
Goose or gosling.

Ortolans.
Small delicate birds; prepared as a table delicacy.

Pain de volaille froid.   Cold chicken loaf.

Pâté d'alouettes.   Lark pie.

Pâté de cailles.   Quail pie.

Pâté de poulet.
Pâté of chicken made with chicken, truffles, brandy, seasoning, forcemeat and enclosed in puff pastry and baked.

Perdreau.   Partridge.

Perdrix.   Partridge.

Pigeonneaux OR **pigeons.**   Squabs.

Poularde.*
A hen or fat pullet especially fattened for the kitchen.

Poularde en brioche.
Chicken baked in yeast dough.

Poularde en chemise.
Poached stuffed chicken.

Poularde à l'estragon.
Chicken prepared with fresh tarragon.

Poularde de grain.*   Spring chicken.

Poularde lyonnaise.
Stuffed chicken cooked with truffles and vegetables.

Poularde Marengo.
Chicken dish made with olive oil, wine, stock, fresh tomatoes or tomato paste, and black olives.

* Strictly speaking *poularde* is a fat pullet, *poularde de grain* is a spring chicken, *poule* is a hen, *poulet* is a chicken, and *poussin* is a very young chicken. All of these terms tend to be used rather loosely for the extensive variety of chicken dishes.

Poularde à la Périgord.
Chicken stuffed with truffles and baked in a glazed sauce.

Poularde au riz.
Well-seasoned chicken garnished with rice.

Poularde strasbourgeoise.
Chicken breasts stuffed with pâté de fois gras.

Poularde à la tartare.
Chicken brushed with olive oil, bread crumbs usually served with a sauce.

Poularde en terrine à la gelée.
Chicken stuffed with forcemeat, prepared in an aspic and usually served on ice for hors d'œuvres or cold buffet.

Poularde vin blanc.   Chicken with white wine.

Poule* au pot.   Chicken in the pot.

Poulet.*   Young chicken.

Poulet amandine.
Chicken cooked in a wine sauce with tomatoes, stock, sour cream and garnished with shredded almonds.

Poulet armagnac.
Chicken cooked in a sauce with armagnac brandy.

Poulet bourguignonne.
Chicken cooked in red wine with onions and mushrooms.

Poulet chasseur.
Chicken sautéed in olive oil, butter, shallots and tomato sauce.

Poulet à la crème.
Chicken in a rich cream sauce.

Poulet dinde.   Baby turkey.

Poulet de grain en casserole.
Spring chicken cooked and served in a casserole; usually in a wine sauce with onions, carrots, turnips, celery, leeks and mushrooms.

Poulet de grain grillé diable.
Broiled deviled spring chicken; sautéed in butter, brushed with mustard, bread crumbs.

Poulet grillé. Grilled chicken.

Poulet à la Kiev.
Boned chicken breasts, stuffed with a finger of sweet butter and fried.

Poulet à la Katoff.
Grilled chicken served on Duchesse potatoes with a rich veal gravy.

Poulet Marengo.
Chicken sautéed in olive oil with wine, mushrooms, stock, tomatoes and olives.

Poulet niçoise.
Chicken cooked with garlic, saffron and tomatoes.

Poulet paysanne. Chicken with vegetables.

Poulet sauté. Chicken lightly cooked in butter.

Poulet sauté aux fines herbes.
Sautéed chicken seasoned with parsley, chevril and tarragon.

Poulet sauté indienne. Curried chicken.

Poulet sauté à la Maintenon.
Sautéed chicken with mushrooms.

Poulet sauté provençale.
Chicken sautéed in olive oil and simmered in a well-seasoned wine sauce with herbs.

Poulet à la Stanley.
Chicken with mushrooms and paprika.

Poussin.* Very young chicken.

Quenelle de volaille. Chicken dumpling.

Salade de poulet. Chicken salad.

Salmis. Birds or game birds stewed in wine.

Sanglier. Boar.

Selle de chevreuil.
Saddle of roebuck; usually served with a sauce.

Soufflé de volaille. Chicken soufflé.

Suprêmes de poulet. Breasts of chicken.

* *See* footnote p. 37.

Suprêmes de volaille aux champignons.
Sautéed chicken breasts served with mushrooms in a
delicately seasoned sauce with varied garnishes.
Suprêmes de volaille jardinière.
Sautéed chicken breasts served with a garnish of fresh
vegetables.
Suprême de volaille parisienne.
Sautéed chicken cooked in a wine sauce and served
with a rich mushroom sauce or hollandaise.
Venado.   Venison.
Vol-au-vent.
Light puff pastry filled with chicken or meat in a rich,
cream sauce.
Yaourt. Yogurt.   A thick, creamy, preparation made
from fermented milk and yeast.

OMELETS

Omelette aux artichauts.
Omelet with artichoke hearts.
Omelette au lard.   Omelet with bacon.
Omelette bonne femme.
Bacon and onion omelet.

Omelette célestine.   Jam omelet.

Omelette aux cèpes.   Sliced mushroom omelet.

Omelette aux champignons.
Mushroom omelet.
Omelette au confiture.   Jam omelet.

Omelette aux crevettes.   Shrimp omelet.

Omelette espangnole.   Spanish omelet.

Omelettes aux fines herbes.
Omelet with finely chopped herbs.

Omelette foies de volaille.
Omelet with sautéed chicken livers.

Omelette au fromage.   Cheese omelet.
Omelette au jambon.   Ham omelet.
Omelette au lard.   Bacon omelet.

Omelette à la lyonnaise.
Omelet with finely minced sautéed onions.

Omelette nature.   Plain omelet.

Omelette aux oignons.   Chopped onion omelet.

Omelette Parmentier.   Diced potato omelet.

Omelette aux pomme de terre.
Potato omelet.

Omelette provençale.
Omelet made with onions, garlic and tomatoes.

Omelette aux rognons.   Kidney omelet.

Omelette à la Rossini.
Omelet made with foie gras and truffles.

Omelette soufflée.
Light, puffed omelet; usually a luncheon or dessert dish.

Omelette aux tomates.   Tomato omelet.

POTATOES

Pommes de terre allemande.
Cooked potatoes, sliced and fried in butter.

Pommes de terre allumettes.
Fried, shoe-string potatoes.

Pommes de terre Alphonse.
Cooked potatoes, sliced and mixed with diced sweet peppers, brushed with maître d'hôtel butter (butter with parsley and dash of lemon juice) and baked with grated cheese.

Pomme de terre à l'anglaise.
Peeled boiled potato.

Pommes de terre Anna.
Sliced potatoes baked and browned in butter in the oven.

Pomme de terre bouillée.   Boiled potato.

Pommes de terre boulangère.
Quartered potatoes baked with minced, sautéed onions.

Pommes de terre "chip."
Thin, crisp fried potato chips.

Pommes de terre à la crème.
Creamed potatoes.

Pommes de terre dauphine.
Sliced potatoes baked with butter and grilled Swiss cheese.

Pommes de terre duchesse.
Boiled potatoes, mashed with egg yolks and butter, shaped into patties and fried or baked.

Pommes de terre farcies.   Stuffed potatoes.

Pommes de terre au four.   Baked potatoes.

Pommes de terre frites.   French fried potatoes.

Pommes de terre hongroise.
Sliced potatoes with onion, paprika, moistened with bouillion and baked.

Pommes de terre au lard.
Potatoes fried with bacon.

Pommes de terre Lorette.
Mashed potatoes mixed with eggs and butter, shaped into crescents and deep fat fried.

Pommes de terre lyonnaise.
Cooked, sliced potatoes sautéed with sliced onions.

Pommes de terre Macaire.
Baked potatoes mashed and prepared in pancake style and browned in an omelet pan of hot butter.

Pommes de terre maître d'hôtel.
Sliced potatoes cooked in milk and served with chopped parsley.

Pommes de terre marquise.
Cooked potatoes with tomato purée shaped into patties and sautéed in butter.

Pommes de terre mousseline.
Cooked mashed potatoes with cream; shaped and glazed.

Pommes de terre nouvelle.   New potatoes.

Pommes de terre parisienne.
Potato balls rolled in a meat glaze and sprinkled with parsley.

Pommes de terre Parmentier.
Sautéed diced potatoes.

Pommes de terre persillées.
Boiled potatoes rolled in melted butter and parsley.

Pommes de terre en purée.   Mashed potatoes.

Pommes de terre rissolées.   Roast potatoes.

Pommes de terre en robe des champs.
Potatoes baked in the jacket.

Pommes de terre sautées.   Sautéed potatoes.

Pommes de terre soufflées.
Very light whipped potatoes.

Pommes de terre surprise.   Baked, stuffed
potatoes.

VEGETABLES AND VEGETABLE DISHES
RICE AND NOODLE DISHES

Abbatis au riz.   Giblets with rice.

Artichauts à la grecque.
Artichokes cooked in herbs and olive oil; usually
served cold.

Asperges au gratin.
Asparagus in a rich creamy cheese sauce and buttered
bread crumbs.

Asperges vinaigrette.
Asparagus with oil and vinegar.

Aubergine.   Eggplant.

Aubergine farcie.   Stuffed, baked eggplant.

Carottes flamandes.   Creamed carrots.

Carottes glacées.   Glazed carrots.

Céleri braisé.   Braised celery.

Céleri rave.
Celery root served as a hot vegetable or a cold hors
d'œuvre in a piquant sauce.

Cèpes à la moelle.
Mushrooms cooked with pieces of marrow.

Cèpes provençale.
Wild meaty mushrooms (bolitus variety) cooked with garlic and tomatoes.

Cèpes sautés à la provençale.
Sautéed mushrooms (bolitus variety) prepared with onions, garlic, tomatoes; provincial style.

Champignons.   Small mushrooms.

Champignons farcis.   Stuffed mushrooms.

Champignons grillés.
Mushrooms grilled in butter.

Chanterelles.   Type of mushroom.

Chou-au-lard.   Cabbage cooked with bacon.

Choucroute garnie.
Hot sauerkraut with meat and sausage.

Chou-fleur à l'huile.
Cauliflower marinated in oil and vinegar; served cold.

Chou de Bruxelles.   Brussels sprouts.

Choux farcis.   Stuffed cabbage.

Cœur de céleri.   Hearts of celery.

Concombre.   Cucumber.

Coquillettes.   Elbow macaroni.

Courgettes niçoise.   Squash with onions and rice.

Endive au jus.   Sautéed endive.

Endive au meunière.   Endive baked in butter.

Épinards en branche.   Spinach cooked in butter.

Épinards à la crème.   Creamed spinach.

Flageolets.   Small kidney beans.

Fonds d'artichauts.   Hearts of artichokes.

Girolle.   Variety of mushroom.

Haricots rouges au vin.
Red beans cooked in wine.

Haricots verts sautés.   Sautéed string beans.

Laitue paysanne.
Lettuce cooked with ham, onions and carrots.

Laitue de printemps braisée au bacon.
Braised lettuce with bacon.

Légumes panachés.   Mixed vegetables.

Macaroni au fromage.   Macaroni with cheese.

Macaroni au gratin.
Macaroni with Béchamel sauce, sprinkled with grated cheese, melted butter and baked.

Macaroni à la Nantua.
Cooked macaroni mixed with crayfish, baked and served in a timbale or mold.

Macédoine de légumes.
Mixture of diced, fresh vegetables.

Nouilles au fromage.   Noodles and cheese.

Petits pois à la française.
Tiny peas cooked with butter, finely minced onion and lettuce.

Petits pois au jambon.
Peas with minced onion and ham.

Petits pois aux laitues.   Peas with lettuce.

Points d'asperges.   Tender, green asparagus tips.

Pois à la française.
Green peas cooked with onions and lettuce.

Purée des légumes.
Creamed preparation of finely chopped vegetables.

Purée St. Germain.   Creamed green peas.

Purée soubise.   Creamed onions.

Ratatouille.
Chopped eggplant, green peppers, tomatoes, onions, garlic and olive oil; a dish of Arabic origin.

Risotto à la turque.
Rice with saffron and tomatoes.

Riz à la créole.
Rice with tomatoes and pimentoes.

Riz à la grecque.
Cooked rice with chopped onion, peas, sweet red pepper and shredded lettuce.

Riz sauvage.   Wild rice.

Riz à la valencienne.
Rice, tomatoes, saffron, onion and shellfish.

Tomates farcies.   Stuffed tomatoes.

Tomates grillées.   Grilled whole tomatoes.

Tomates sautées à la provençale.
Seasoned sliced tomatoes sautéed in olive oil with garlic, garnished with parsley and bread crumbs and baked.

Truffles.
Type of fungus that thrives underground, considered a true delicacy. Can be used as an hors d'œuvre or vegetable but more usually a garnish.

Truffles au champagne.
Truffles in champagne sauce; served in a pastry crust.

Truffles à la crème.
Truffles in rich cream sauce and brandy; served in light pastry crust.

SALADS

French salads are varied but quite simple in preparation. Dressings are added in small quantities and garlic is used very sparingly; perhaps the secret of French salad excellence is that it is mixed directly before serving.

Salade de betterave.
Thinly sliced beet salad with finely chopped herbs.

Salade caprice.
Similar to a chef's salad; that is various kinds of lettuce with a julienne of tongue, ham, chicken and artichoke hearts.

Salade de céleri.   Hearts of celery.

Salade de chicorée aux tomates.
Chicory and tomato salad.

Salade de chou rouge.   Red cabbage salad.

Salade de chou.   Coleslaw.

Salade de concombres.
Thinly sliced cucumbers with oil, vinegar and chervil.

Salade de cresson.   Watercress salad.

Salade cressonnière.
Salad mixture of potatoes, watercress, parsley, chervil and hard-boiled egg.

Salade d'haricots sec et de lentilles.
Haricot beans and lentil salad with thinly sliced onion.

Salade d'haricots verts. String bean salad.

Salade italienne.
Assortment of raw or cooked vegetables with salami, anchovies, olives and capers with mayonnaise dressing.

Salade de laitue et betteraves.
Lettuce and beet root salad.

Salade de légumes.
Freshly cooked vegetable salad with oil and vinegar dressing.

Salade de lentilles.
Salad of cold boiled lentils, well seasoned.

Salade niçoise.
Salad of string beans, diced potatoes, tomatoes, olives, anchovies and hard-boiled eggs served with oil and vinegar.

Salade panachée au cresson.
Mixed salad with watercress.

Salade de pissenlit. Dandelion salad.

Salade de poireau. Leek salad.

Salade de pomme de terre. Potato salad.

Salade de romaine à l'estragon.
Salad of romaine lettuce with fresh tarragon.

Salade russe.
Mixture of cooked vegetables, ham, lobster; all cut julienne style and mixed with mayonnaise.

Salade de saison. Salad of the season.

Salade de scarole aux fines herbes.
Escarole salad with finely chopped herbs.

Salade de tomatoes.
Sliced tomatoes served in a tasty mixture of oil, vinegar and herbs.

Salade verte. Mixed green salad.

Saladier. Salad bowl.

CHEESE

Beaufort de Savoie.
Similar to Swiss gruyere; made of cow's milk.
Bonvillois.   Soft, creamy white cheese.
Brie.
Round, flat, creamy white cheese; made with cow's milk.
Cabrion.   Goat's milk cheese.
Cachat.   Cheese made with ewe's milk in Provence.
Camembert.
Creamy, ripe cheese; made with cow's milk in Normandy.
Cantal.   Small, hard cheese; made in Auvergne.
Chabris.   Goat's milk cheese.
Chèvre. Chèvreton. Chevrotin. Chevrotton.
Goat's milk cheese; made in many varieties, sizes and shapes.
Coulommiers.
Creamy, sharp cow's milk cheese; from the Île de France region.
Crème Chantilly.   Creamy, mild dessert cheese.
Demi-sel.
Light cream cheese made with cow's milk.
Dreux.   Soft-textured cheese made with cow's milk.
Emmenthal.
Gruyère cheese with holes; from the Emme valley.
Fontainbleau.   Cream cheese.
Forez.   Similar to Roquefort cheese.
Fromage. blanc.   Cottage cheese.
Fromage à la crème.   Cream cheese.
Fromage de chèvre.   Goat's milk cheese.
Fromage de Hollande.
Dutch cheese; usually refers to Edam.
Géromé.   Sharp cheese made with cow's milk.
Marlieu.   Round, mild, white cheese.
Neufchâtel.   Mild, creamy cheese from Normandy.
Olivet.   Soft cheese from Orléans.
Persillé.   Similar to Roquefort.

Petit suisse. Cream cheese.

Pont l'Evêque. Semi-hard cheese from Normandy.

Port-du-Salut OR **Port Salut.**
Soft, smooth cheese with distinctive flavor.

Providence. Similar to Port-du-Salut.

Reblochon.
Soft whole milk cheese; from the Loire valley.

Roquefort.
Sharp, pungent, blue-veined cheese made with ewe's milk, and well aged.

Septmoncel. Hard cheese similar to Roquefort.

Suisse. Swiss cheese.

Trouville. Similar to Pont l'Evêque.

Vendôme. Similar to Camembert.

DESSERTS

Africains. Small dessert cookies.

Ananas au kirsch.
Pineapple steeped in kirsch liqueur.

Assiette de friandises.
Assortment of fancy cookies.

Baba au rhum. Light yeast cake soaked in rum.

Biscuits.
Biscuits or delicate cookies usually served with ice cream.

Bombe.
Mould of ice cream, whipped cream and fruit; or several flavors of ice cream combined.

Bugne. Doughnut.

Café viennois. Coffee ice cream with whipped cream.

Cerises jubilée.
Brandied cherries served aflame over ice cream.

Chantilly. Whipped cream.

Charlotte Malakoff.
Rich, creamy dessert made with lady fingers, whipped cream and almonds.

Compote.   Stewed fruit in light syrup.

Cornet de glace.   Ice cream cone.

Corbeille de fruits.   Basket of fruit.

Coupe favorite.
Ice cream flavored with kirsch, garnished with whipped cream and strawberry purée.

Coupe glacée.
Ice cream topped with whipped cream; similar to the American sundae.

Coupe (St.) Jacques.
Ices or ice cream heaped with a macédoine of fresh fruit in kirsch.

Crème caramel.   Light caramel cream pudding.

Crème Chantilly.   Whipped cream with sugar.

Crêpes au sucre.   Thin pancakes served with sugar.

Crêpes Suzette.
Thin pancakes steeped in a sauce made with butter, sugar, oranges, liqueurs and brandy, flamed in a chafing dish.

Café liégeois.
Coffee ice cream with whipped cream.

Dartois.
Cake made of light puff pastry usually filled with pastry cream or jelly.

Diplomate.
Cold pudding made with crushed fruit and whipped cream.

Doigt de dame.   Meringue lady fingers.

Éclair.   Éclair filled with whipped cream or custard.

Éclair au café.   Coffee éclair.

Éclair au chocolat.   Chocolate éclair.

Fraises à la crème.
Fresh strawberries served with sugar and cream.

Fraises des bois.
Small very fresh wild strawberries.

Fraises Romanoff.
Strawberries steeped in orange juice and curaçoa with ice cream or whipped cream.

Framboises.   Fresh wild raspberries.

Fruits frais.   Fresh fruit.

Galette bretonne.
Round, flat tasty cookie made in Brittany.

Gâteau.
Cake.   Gateau de maison is the cake specialty of the house.

Gâteau d'amande.   Almond cake.

Génoise.
Smooth-textured yellow cake used for petits fours and sponge rolls.

Glace.   Ice cream or ices.

Glace à la vanille.   Vanilla ice cream.

Glace au chocolat.   Chocolate ice cream.

Glace aux fraises.   Strawberry ice cream.

Glace aux fruits.
Ice cream with crushed fruit or fruit syrup.

Glace napolitaine.   Combination of ices and ice cream.

Glace panachée.   Mixed ice cream.

Granité.   Ices with fruit syrup.

Liégeois.   Soft ice cream dessert.

Macédoine de fruits.
Mixture of fresh fruits and liqueur.

Madeleine.   Small butter cookie.

Marignan.   Sponge cake filled with whipped cream.

Marquise.   Ices with whipped cream.

Marrons glacés.   Candied chestnuts.

Massepain.
Colorful and decorative candy-like cookies made with almonds, sugar, eggs and flavoring.

Mazarin.
Yeast cake with kirsch liqueur and sabayon sauce.

Melba.
Dessert sauce made with raspberries, currant jelly, lemon juice and sugar.

Melon glacé.   Cold melon.

Melon frappé. Iced melon with liqueur.

Meringue. Confection of egg whites and sugar.

Meringue glacées.
Ice cream in a swirl of baked egg white.

Mille-feuille.
Flaky puff pastry used as a tart or for cookies.

Mirabelles. Small yellow plums.

Moka. Pastry with mocha cream frosting.

Mont Blanc.
Fruit or chestnut purée with flavored whipped cream.

Mousse.
Light sweet dessert made with whipped cream and lightly beaten eggs.

Mousse au chocolat. Chocolate mousse.

Mousse de fraises. Strawberry mousse.

Napoléon.
Whipped cream or light custard sandwiched between flaky layers of delicate pastry.

Nesselrode.
Sauce or tart filling made with brandied fruits and chestnuts in a rich syrup.

Nougat.
Confection of almonds, pistachio nuts, honey and sugar.

Omelette flambée au rhum.
Omelet served with flamed rum sauce and powdered sugar.

Parfait.
Any combination of ice cream, whipped cream, fruits served in a tall glass.

Pâtisserie. General term for pastry.

Pêche Melba.
Vanilla ice cream with peaches and crushed raspberry syrup.

Petit sablé. Cookies.

Petits fours.
Small cakes or cookies.

Petits pots de crème.
Cold custard dessert prepared in many different flavors and served in small traditional French crocks.

Poire cardinal.
Stewed pears with raspberry sauce and toasted almonds.
Poire Hélène.
Stewed pears with vanilla ice cream and chocolate sauce.
Pomme au beurre.   Baked apple.
Pomme bonne femme.   Baked apple.
Pot au crème.
Custard dessert served in traditional crock.
Pouding.   Pudding.
Profiterole.
Small, flaky pastry filled with custard, ice cream or whipped cream usually served with chocolate sauce.
Pudding de cabinet.
Pudding made with candied fruits, raisins, liqueur and lady fingers.
Pudding de riz.   Rice pudding.
Pudding soufflé.
Light, fluffy pudding made with stiffly beaten egg whites.
Riz impératrice.
Rice pudding with candied fruit and whipped cream; served cold.
Sablés.   Small, tasty cookies.
Savarin.
Rum-soaked sponge cake served with fruit and garnished with whipped cream.
Sorbet.   Sherbet.
Soufflé.
Egg yolks, stiffly beaten whites and an extensive variety of fruit, flavors, syrups are the basic ingredients for a favorite dessert or entrée.   Served cold or hot and sometimes flamed.
Soufflé au chocolat.   Chocolate soufflé.
Soufflé aux liqueurs.
Soufflé flavored distinctively with a particular liqueur.
Soufflé à la vanille.   Vanilla soufflé.
Stanislas.   Cake with almond cream filling.
Tarte.   Open pastry shell filled with fruit or custard.

Tarte aux fraises. Strawberry tart.

Tartelettes. Little tarts filled with fruit or custard.

Tranche napolitaine.
Ice cream slice of several flavors.

Tranche plombières. Ice cream with fruit.

Vacherin. Meringue shell filled with whipped cream.

BEVERAGES

Cacoa. Cocoa.

Café. Coffee.

Café brûlot. Coffee with sugar and flaming brandy.

Café complet.
Refers to continental breakfast consisting of coffee with hot milk, rolls, jam and butter.

Café crème. Coffee with cream.

Café diable.
Coffee with cinnamon, cloves, sugar, orange rind and flaming brandy.

Café double. Double-strength coffee.

Café filtre. Strong drip coffee.

Café frappé OR **glacé.** Iced coffee.

Café au lait. Coffee with hot milk.

Café nature OR **noir.** Black coffee.

Café soluble. Instant coffee.

Orange pressé. Fresh fruit orangeade.

Thé. Tea.

INDEX

The numbers following all Index entries refer to *item numbers*, except for major section entries which are in capitals and refer to *page number*.